NO
BIGG
DEAL!
(AN MT SALES STORY)

Rasal

Edited by: Bilawal

Chennai • Bangalore

CLEVER FOX PUBLISHING
Chennai, India

Published by CLEVER FOX PUBLISHING 2023
Copyright © Rasal 2023

All Rights Reserved.
ISBN: 978-93-56484-76-4

This book has been published with all reasonable efforts taken to make the material error-free after the consent of the author. No part of this book shall be used, reproduced in any manner whatsoever without written permission from the author, except in the case of brief quotations embodied in critical articles and reviews.

The Author of this book is solely responsible and liable for its content including but not limited to the views, representations, descriptions, statements, information, opinions and references ["Content"]. The Content of this book shall not constitute or be construed or deemed to reflect the opinion or expression of the Publisher or Editor. Neither the Publisher nor Editor endorse or approve the Content of this book or guarantee the reliability, accuracy or completeness of the Content published herein and do not make any representations or warranties of any kind, express or implied, including but not limited to the implied warranties of merchantability, fitness for a particular purpose. The Publisher and Editor shall not be liable whatsoever for any errors, omissions, whether such errors or omissions result from negligence, accident, or any other cause or claims for loss or damages of any kind, including without limitation, indirect or consequential loss or damage arising out of use, inability to use, or about the reliability, accuracy or sufficiency of the information contained in this book.

A THANK-YOU NOTE

We all have Angelos in our lives. Ones who come from nowhere, do their angelic bit, before vanishing to nowhere. Not waiting for a word of gratitude, or even a goodbye. Sometimes forcing us to write a whole book instead of that one 'thank you' we missed to say in time.

Without further ado ...

CONTENTS

A Thank-you Note iii

1. Guilty As Charged: Virgin, Charmless 1
2. The Unsettling Setting 7
3. The Unwilling Salesman 12
4. A Disorientation Pogrom 20
5. The Red-letter Day 28
6. Another Forced Baptism; No Cries 35
7. The Sales Failures 47
8. Sales Failures Continued 58
9. Monday Again, but Why? 68
10. An Angelo Descends 76
11. An Office, Two Boards 81
12. A Man, Many Words, Dirty Secrets 87
13. Sales Wins Continue, but Why? 94
14. A Good Samart Arrives 104
15. A Beautiful Promise (Almost). The End (Almost) 108
16. A Beautiful Promise That Never Was 114

Contents

17. An Interlude before the Actual End 118
18. And 'The End' That Was to Be 132

A Thank-you Note (Continued) 135
Postscript 137
About the Author 139

GUILTY AS CHARGED: VIRGIN, CHARMLESS

*E*ver been a virgin? A beginner? A trainee? A sheep among the lions? A novice among the masters? That ominous first day; the palpitations. Untrained, unproven, unsure ... Pushed off the cliff on a leap of faith with no visible harnesses, yet you refuse to be *fallen*. Thrown into the deep end with no floatation aids, yet you refuse to be *sunk*. Are you one who has made it across, now wondering how you managed to? Are you one currently lost in an abyss, wondering what next? Curious to know how it is for another even as you drown. To find that very human joy in knowing how others also suffer, forgetting our sufferings for a few indulgent moments. Are you one about to be pushed off?

Okay. Are you at least someone who is not *dead*, yet? If yes, I have a story to share ...

Yet another of those familiar Friday evening meetings where brains get stormed, fingers get pointed, bucks get passed and teas get drunk. The ideal culmination to a week one wished never happened. The ideal start to a weekend fraught with Saturday and Sunday blues. Then, it is Monday morning all over again. Then, the mourning starts. The blues assume darker hues. That most hated day of the week, the world over. Isn't it so? Or am I wrong, again? Are there real humans who love Monday mornings? You do?

'The problem with Mehraz is a clear lack of interest.' Thomas, the bespectacled wise one, was the first to weigh in with his wise thoughts. 'No enthusiasm, almost lifeless at times. Meh, as the name goes. Ours is not a trade where one sits behind the desk, fully decked, expecting patrons to walk to us. One has to get out on the road and get dirty. That is where the action is.' An intelligent remark. An intelligent grin. It flashes. It fades.

'Yes, I agree. The other issue with Mehraz is this constant harping on *long term*, as if it is some sort of marriage, you know. Our clients are mostly older people, never easy to get them excited about anything. We got to find a way to pique their interest, at least for a short while. Then, those abandoned husbands of non-residents: the *Left-behinds*. They are rich, young and open to new things. But this one might not be able to find a way to get through to them. Maybe someone with more charm, you know …' J. U. Das, the compulsive *concurrer* and occasional backstabber, readily concurred. Having given words to his resentment for this new uninvited presence in their midst, he then looked around for concurrence. As always, his eyes ended transfixed on the Pretty One.

The Pretty One, as always, gave the impression that she was so full of words, about to say something, smiled a pretty smile and went back to being ensconced in a bubble of expectant silence. And continued to look pretty. A beautiful mannequin that cannot talk.

'It's unfair to write someone off this early. This one is just getting started and we know that they always take time. Let us be patient. The Lord shall show us a way.' As always, the sympathetic elderly lady's words were mild, true, and ignored. Mini, her name. Mini *Chechi* as Meh and the others used to call her. [*Chechi:* elder sister]

As is the case everywhere, the buck ended with the antagonistic Chief. Shibu. That is his name, by the way. In this Land of Letters, they go totally lazy with people's names. Two syllables: *Sheee* and a *Buuu*. That's it! Christened. Baptised. Done. The kind of name that gives the impression that something is to follow, leaves the listener with ears sharpened and head half tilted in anticipation of what is to follow, but nothing ever does. Shibu was everything that a man his age does around here to be respectable, and fails.

A dyed walrus moustache, as if he is biting obstinately on to a frayed paintbrush dripping with black paint. That familiar strong smell of cheap *attar*, one that every man's every brother-in-law gets from every possible country in the Persian Gulf. A potbelly always in a hurry to get ahead of himself, arrives everywhere before Shibu does, right after the perfume smell, giving everyone time to settle in their seats and appear serious by the time the rest of Shibu walks in. The perfume then blends in with the office air. The man never does. This marsupial tummy is always painstakingly tucked into a trouser that struggles to touch the ankles, as if there is an imminent flood that he alone has been warned about. On special occasions, like the meeting today, he wears a cheap red nylon tie, too. Again, intended to lend him an air of respectability and professionalism. It lent him neither.

'Yes, I know. This one is totally useless in this trade. As useless a *virgin* as they come. Wish we had a pro. Anyway, let bygones be bygones. We will start afresh from Monday. I have a plan in mind.' Shibu signed off the charge sheet.

Anyone who eavesdrops on this conversation, as you just did, will be forgiven for having failed to guess that this is an exchange from an insurance sales review meeting. In a trade that shares dubiously faint borders with some less respectable ones, this is how it usually goes, making one wonder what really gets plied behind closed doors. The problem was readily identified, almost unanimously. Only a solution remained pending.

We all wait until Monday for that.

Mehraz—referred to above as Meh, the virgin, the lifeless, the charmless, the useless; that unanimous problem—stood riveted to a corner, back against the wall, witnessing this weekly routine of charges levelled, egos hurt and hopes deflated ... all suffered in silence. Then everyone else enthusiastically moved on to the next item on the agenda, almost as enjoyable as the young man's weekly humiliation—the frothy Kerala *ttttea* and the flaky egg *pufffffs*. We love our teas and our word stresses, all at the wrong times. Damn proud too.

Mehraz sneaked out, exchanging glances with Shibu. He saw an evil smirk transform into a laboured smile on Shibu's face, just as it does with everyone in this land. It appeared more animated with a sticky flake of the puff pastry perched precariously on the wickedly longer end of his cynical smirk.

The flight of stairs exited onto the crossroads that had the ever-reliable *paanwala* by the side. He seemed to be the only man in that town who would offer Mehraz a smile without the fear of it being perceived as a promise. That reassuring presence at every crossroad. *Sutta* on the mint *dabba* ... *chutta* on the *chikki dabba* ... loose change returned ... broad smiles exchanged. If only all buyer-seller relationships in this land were as uncomplicated as that between the cigarette vendor and his patrons who bought death with a smile! Why is it that selling this darn death insurance alone so complicated? Even this comes with its own set of disclaimers, warnings and stuff (less graphic, but no less grave). Doesn't it?

Mehraz left his car behind, along with his usual appendage of a black attaché case that had all the burdens of his present life chaotically dumped in. He lit a cigarette, began walking behind its burning glow, hoping to be led on his path; from darkness to light.

'Send out your light and truth; let them lead me.'

'*Tamasoma jyotir …*'

THE UNSETTLING SETTING

The glow of the cigarette cut through the darkness of that town, guiding Mehraz on his restless walk to nowhere. Thoughts, fleeting like sights, whizzed past as he walked, like the deserted shops by the roadside that were as deserted as they were dimly lit. The roads, in turn, were as wide as they were dark. Wide and dark enough to be filled with people and streetlights, but always devoid of both. You have to bring your own light, or cigarettes.

The domino that someone had set into motion in the past has been falling, pushing Mehraz from one chaotic chequered box into another. And it continues. Finally, to this one town that he never imagined he would ever end up being in after a management degree. He was never sure what he needed to do in life. But if there was one thing he was sure not to do, it was this: Sales. And sales is all that he has to do now. Perhaps for the rest of his life. But wasn't it so with everything else? He never wanted to go to school. Everyone else did, so did he. He never wanted to study well, yet he did. He never wanted to be the compliant son his mother wished him to be, yet he did. All his friends went for a management course, so did he. Almost everyone got a job in sales, so did he. Inscrutable moves. Invisible strings. An ingratiating puppet.

Is it only for him? Is it the same for others too? For Shibu? For you? Is it all by design or by default? Or is it that even the defaults are by a grand design?

The thoughts died down; the cigarette, too. The town looked darker without the glow of cigarette.

This place has always been inexplicably dark, even during daytime. Darkness incarnates into a person here: a pervasive figure; it solidifies into an object at times: a very palpable one. And it gets intensified by lifeless rubber trees that cast a depressing shadow over an entire town and its people. These trees, like everything else in this town, barely move. It is as if no wind ever blows here. A whiff of fresh air? *Never!* It has a pall of solemn gloom hanging over it always, like the unsettling backdrop to a mournful play. Its people love these trees, revere and devour them, like how they love their bovines. For the milk—**Latex** as it is known, the first of the Three Ls— and for the money these lactating trees bring. Once about to dry off permanently, these trees are also *hacked* down in what is called slaughtering. Born, raised and killed for human indulgence, like cows. Cash crops. Cash cows.

The Unsettling Setting

Other than Latex, this is also the land of **Letters** with some of the oldest publishing and newspaper houses having originated here. This is also the land of **Lakes** that are polluted and fast drying up. Thus, making it the Land of Three Ls—Latex, Letters and Lakes. Kottayam: A sleepy little place that sends a lot of rubber, spices and real street-smart people to many parts of the world. A good number of them are nurses, for some odd reason.

The story of Kottayam is only a sub-story in the story of the state of Kerala. A tiny state in the southwestern tip of India that holds an important position, geographically and historically. Or historic because of the geography. Maybe. This is where Europeans had landed and 'discovered' India, as many in Europe still believe. Unaware that the country, and the state, has had trade relations with the world for long: a thriving export of indigo, spices and of what was once called Oriental wisdom, including to the Occident of yesteryears. When most other countries had no worthy exports and had zero clue on how to even describe it, this one gave the confused world the Zero, too. Gave nothingness, taught emptiness; then, the difference between the two.

The state had offered a red-carpet welcome to an apostle who brought Christianity with him, even before it took roots in Europe. Accorded equal status as the gods of this land, his idol taken for temple processions along with other resident deities, he was in august company.

Its people never minded an extra one among their multitude. One mythological personal god for every man at one point before humans started focusing on creating their own progeny and not so much on creating further gods. (And always twice as many god-men, too.) The state had given an early asylum to the diasporic Jews and remained a safe home over millennia. This is also where the peaceful version of Islam had spread to India. Not through invaders who came on horseback with swords to slay, shields to defend, and a holy book in defence. It came with travelling merchants and their teachers. By the word, not by the sword. Through teachers, not invaders.

Thus all major religions have coexisted peacefully and enjoyed all the prosperity that came with the peace. Or the reverse. They competed with each other to set up educational institutions to offer secular as well as sectarian education—an inordinately high literacy rate being its happy by-product. This is also the first major state where a communist government had come to power through ballots and not bullets. Mao had fallen off his dictatorial chair laughing onto a heap of skeletons outside an overfilled closet that day. He then took a *giant leap backwards* and dragged a nation and half a billion people with him in the process. Oddly, it remains the last Indian state that still has a democratic communist government in power.

The Unsettling Setting

To this day, the state remains a hotbed of politics and religion. They continue to feed on each other for survival, contributing to the development of the state most of the time, and at times, to its destruction. One plays the peacemaker when the other goes on a rampage. Thus, these two ugly conjoined twins with shared arms and tentacles, arms and ammunitions, caste and cadre, and everything associated remain deeply entrenched in every aspect of life here. For every enthusiastic explorer once eager to reach its mysterious shores searching for hidden treasures, today, there are thousands desperately leaving its shores, searching for employment. Now people come here for vacations, or for funerals. Mostly. Never for employment. Mostly.

... And as educated people rush to leave this land on airplanes and dhows, trains and trucks, and out of desire and despair, for Mehraz, the domino has fallen into this chequered box. For now. Thus, on a fateful day, he had exited onto a railway platform that always has more people desperate to get on to a train to wherever, than there are people happy to get off.

It was the day of yet another *hartal*.

THE UNWILLING SALESMAN

*T*he Friday evening's desultory walk reached its abortive end in front of a rusty gate of a rented house. That is another thing with this town. It is small; so small that even a directionless walk will take one right to one's home. There are not many places to go to, even to get lost.

An old, decrepit *tharavadu* house with tiled roof, it had a large mango tree right in front. Mango blossoms and squirrels abounded all through the year, but there were no mangoes any time of the year. The blossoms bloomed into innumerable tiny rodents with mystical stripes, Mehraz believed. The squirrels were not shy like how they usually are; they took no efforts to hide themselves. Hysterical, they ran around the courtyard unabashedly, squeaking and chirping incessantly. A twenty-seven thousand three hundred and sixty-four, Meh counted. And on many a moonless night he had seen some of them sprout wings and turn into bats and hang from the higher branches; upside down. Miniature yogis, hanging mid-air. And when the light of his cigarettes went out, he would see their wings disintegrate into darkness and turn back into squirrel-shaped silhouettes of fur … *Sathyam!* He swears.

The house belonged to a large traditional family that once had over twenty members. It is easy to guess what happened to those twenty and their descendants or how such a big house can remain so desolate. Airplanes and dhows. These houses have a charm that no concrete houses have and Meh always loved them; dilapidated buildings with banyan seedlings sprouting out of tiny womb cracks. The more dilapidated, the better. It is as if these houses speak to him. The walls, the well; the rafters, the attic. All hiding large treasure chests of stories. Like an old grandmother who has seen it all, and now has only never-ending stories to offer.

About lost people. About lost glory. About losses alone.

The house is at Kanjikkuzhy, literally translates to 'gruel hole'—the lifeless rice gruel that is reserved for the weak and the poor, that too in a hole—and sort of sums up Meh's current existence. And it remains a cruel irony that he had to choose this place, of all. But this is also the upmarket part of that town along with the adjacent Devalokam, meaning world of celestial beings, that incidentally has the Bishop's House too. Stuck between the gruel hole and demigods, Meh called his father, the *demi-writer* and *semi-philosopher*.

'Do what makes you happy ...' Then there was a pause and an extended silence. The pause was longer than the words the man spoke and as if he suddenly remembered even the pauses cost him money—it was the days of incoming call charges and per-second billing—the father abruptly hung up.

'No but ... listen, *Vappa* ... what to ... wait a sec ... hello ...' *Poyaa ingeru!*

The incorporeal voice had vanished by then. Meh called back.

'See ... told you already. It is demeaning to ask people for money or for favours. I can't imagine my son doing it. Speak to your bosses to try and get a change in role. And if it reaches a stage where it kills the soul, then quit. Here, talk to your mother.'

'Wait! Kill the what?' There has to be something abstract in everything this man says, even to a 23-year-old. Meh tried to process everything else, ignoring the last part; ignoring the soul. And he continued to ignore it, for many years to come.

Mother came on the line. 'Did you have dinner, Meh? Please do not worry. Why do you go for all this? I have been telling you about that junior professor's vacancy in my college. You come back. You are too good a boy to be selling anything or cheating anyone. [Both in the same breath. Charmless and harmless.] I know you, I raised you. Listen to me, Meh; no harm will come to you.'

'Sure, *Amma*.' The call dropped on its own.

No harm will come, but no good will come either. What good does a man learn, he who makes no mistakes? Let me at least start making my own mistakes. I may be too good for sales. Perhaps not good enough for sales. But what am I good for? What will make me happy? How many 23-year-olds know it? How many 43-year-olds do? Meh wondered.

How many wrong roles before we get to know the role we should be playing? How many years of this pain of pretending to be someone we know we are not? A pain that a man would know if he were to get trapped inside a woman's body. Even as you pretend to be a woman for the world, deep within, you know that it isn't you. That there is a being within struggling for expression. A pain with a purpose, they say. A pain alone that you will know, never the purpose. Does everyone feel this sort of pain? This burning desire for expression? Or was it him alone?

The charades. The masquerades. A never-ending costume party …

No Bigg Deal!

A quick shower. That only meant one thing: stepping out. Then, alcohol. At Hotel Ambassador. Most of the working days of a sales guy are bad. Uninterested and unreasonable prospects, unsatisfactory meetings that never go as desired, unattended wives and unsatisfied bosses, unachievable targets and elusive incentives, more promises and fewer cheques to show for it. Throw in some Shibus in between ... Real Bad! And in the evening, everything changes. Ethanol has to be the favourite chemical—of every optimistic alchemist, of every distressed man. Suddenly, people are not that bad, meetings are just about perfect, targets can still be met, incentives and amends can always be made; and after all, what is life without hopes and promises. Shibu? No, he remains a pain even after all the alcohol. It makes everything (else) look good for one night and at the end of the Cinderella hour, one wakes up for an encore of the previous day, with the hope of an encore of the previous night. A depressing loop.

After alcohol, there is always that morbid desire for flesh. That carnal sin! The walk through a dark alleyway that takes him to a place where craving for flesh is satiated every night. Seductive temptations make their way into a darkened hall with sooty bulbs and dirty curtains conjured out of discarded *lungis*, wafting past aromatic smoke curtains of a cloudy kitchen. Kerala *porotta*, *Achayan's* beef fry and pork roast. At Hobnob restaurant. One meal, multiple sins. A Muslim father, a Hindu mother offended. A few million gods plus one omnipotent affronted. All in one shot. All with one meal. How easy it is these days—to confuse, to sin; to upset, to offend. Humans. Gods. Rules.

Shortly, back in the room, the final cigarette for the day was put out along with a flickering bulb. Then there was bright darkness. Enough darkness that one could sleep with one's eyes open, yet he couldn't. The thing with alcohol is that it enlivens the mind for some, making them full of thoughts and life. They never get sleep, a high, or a hangover. It does the opposite of what it does to most people. Meh got down on the floor and lay on his side, legs drawn close to his chest, ear to the ground. As if he wanted to listen to what Mother Earth had to tell him. As if he wished for a foetal bowl of darkness to be formed around him and keep him safe and hidden in it, away from the world. As if he wished to lose himself totally in that darkness.

In your darkest hours, when even your shadow abandons you, you begin to find your strength in that sort of solitude. A flame within that lights your path as you find your way in that darkness. One thing that can upset that flame is ... a sudden overseas call from a girlfriend who needs an answer to be conveyed to her father. Today was the deadline for that, too. Missing deadlines is, by now, a part of Meh's life.

There was not much sign of life inside that old house, except for the constant nagging of a possessive girlfriend on phone and the occasional buzzing of an inquisitive lone female mosquito that shared the house with Mehraz. Only one of them he counted a companion in that house. Only one of them he took particular care not to offend. Only one of them he did not wish to bludgeon to death with a rolled-up newspaper. And only one of them he did not even mind marrying. Give a drop of blood and one was happy. The other never needed a reason to be sad. She never could find reasons to be happy either. She was the only one always baying for more, Meh felt.

He turned the phone to silent and curled up on the floor again. He then felt he needed a warm hug. For someone to hold him tight so that the crumbling parts of his self are squeezed back together. To keep it from falling apart. Every desire of the human body can easily be fulfilled, either through someone or even on your own. You can always caress and fondle, excite and satiate yourself. But no one can ever hug oneself. For that you need another, with a warm heart. Meh wondered how helpless and dependent human beings are. He wondered if others also felt the same way. A powerless insomniac with fanciful dreams even while awake. He tossed and turned: a sinner in a cursed dark grave. Sleep eluded him that night. The mosquito, too. An overheated phone kept vibrating on silent mode. Buzzing like a disgruntled mosquito in a faraway country.

Since weekends were as lifeless as weekdays in that town and with no one ever wanting to meet him willingly, there were no scheduled appointments for the next two days. He threw some clothes into a bag and prepared to leave for the neighbouring city. On a train. There was some semblance of life and some friends there. And as it happens in most cities and with most people living his kind of life, life happened there on those two days at least. For people who choose to live only two-seventh of their lives, surrendering the rest of their lives to making a living. Then life appears to happen, after having put it on hold for five days.

Everything can wait for two days. He will deal with all his problems on Monday morning, like everyone else. Including Shibu's big plan for Monday.

A train—that again had not many wanting to exit—pulled into a dark station in the dead of the night …

A DISORIENTATION POGROM

𝓑ut didn't Mehraz major in marketing and not in sales? How did he end up being in this place? How did he end up being the charmless salesman? Well, marketing is only a euphemism for sales, for most. Marketing jobs are reserved for the lucky few and dubious sales jobs get rebranded and marketed as marketing jobs to aspiring marketers: your first practical lesson in packaging, branding and selling the spurious.

Insurance was touted as the 'sunrise' sector in a country that was already 'shining,' borrowing the flame from a campaign that the government was using to market itself. Those days it was marketing everywhere: countries, states, governments, politicians, spiritual gurus, film stars. Campus recruits, fondly called Management Trainees (MTs), are to be future CEOs. They are promised stints in all divisions of an organisation before they become CEOs. That was the first and most recurring lie in a

A Disorientation Pogrom

series of lies they parroted, starting with the recruiting manager who had come to campus; like kidnappers luring unsuspecting kids from school gates. A gullible child, never forewarned enough to say, 'I do not know you,' baited successfully. That promised sweet candy of job rotation is a sham; it never happens. Their careers start in sales and end in sales, or in heart attacks. Like how it happens in the all-too-familiar human trafficking stories from the rich Arab countries where promised plush jobs end up with the drudgery of being a *Gaddhama*—Arabic for housemaid—or a camel washer, or a male slave of a raunchy *Arabab:* the boss. Sales jobs are the *Gaddhama* equivalent for most marketing graduates.

All the disoriented new recruits were then herded in for an orientation programme. This is where the brainwashing starts. Glitzy hotels, glowing propaganda. Contrary to what he was always told to believe, there were free lunches in that world, Meh noticed. Then in a marketing training session that followed, they mentioned, 'If you are not paying for a product, remember, you are the product.' Meh noticed that, too.

What followed was an insightful lecture on competition in insurance and the lengths insurance companies go to, to get creative and destructive with their marketing campaigns. (An apocryphal story that is so common in that world, every insurance company loves to usurp it, choosing to be the second company. No one is known to have ever volunteered to be the first company.) It had happened in the U.S., as it does with all things apocryphal.

When the first company came out with an advertisement to highlight the scope of its coverage across various life stages, its tagline read:

'From cradle to grave.'

This was the first salvo in a series of escalating creative salvos, the trainer gleamed. The second company was forced to come up with something more creative and comprehensive in response, which they did:

'From womb to tomb.'

The tone had been set and the defeated marketing team, forced to storm their creative brains, came up with a befitting retort:

'From sperm to worm.' Voilà! Pure gold.

Just when the first company and its creative heads assumed no human brain can go any further or deeper, some great minds at the second company fired the last salvo that is yet to be bettered by any insurance company anywhere in the world:

'From erection to resurrection.'

'Brilliant, brilliant, and brilliant!' The trainer screamed like a passionate preacher. Hallelujah!

'That, my dear friends, is what we expect from you all. That creativity. That aggression. That killer instinct. That willingness to fire a bazooka even on a lamb. This is war. There are no losers here, only winners and the dead. And dear friends, that insurance company with the greatest marketing campaign ever, the gold standard for insurance marketing the world over, is our own Con Ass Inc. [Continental Assurance Incorporated]; the greatest. The proud legacy that you all need to live up to.' The man stood levitated on an elevated platform on raised toes, with raised neck hair, and arms spread like the Christ the Redeemer statue. A fat thumb then flicked into oblivion a pregnant teardrop, remained raised, as if in self-approbation. A second drop retreated itself, in embarrassment.

Lights back on. Thunderous applause filled the room.

Meh was looking for the free *chaai biskoot*. He took pains to not make eye contact with anyone and focused on dunking the *biskoot* in the *chaai* without it falling off. *Blummm! Plonk!* He could not. He peered through a furtive gap between a pair of inquiring brows and a thick glass rim to see if anyone noticed. He wondered if anyone in this country ever managed to do it right.

In between free lunches and *chaai*, everyone was well fed with successful sales stories. Stories of great men who had achieved sales greatness, sewn into shady videos that were played incessantly. Like videos of the Kim Jongs to North Koreans. Some see right through it. They know that these swanky rooms, the comforts, the full plates are all equally staged. That it is all Pyongyang recreated in its corporate version and they remain unconvinced. Many feel an enthusiasm that lasts a few days or months. The chosen few feel it for many years and they keep this cycle going; ones who love Mondays more than Fridays. Workaday indulgences.

They call this initial phase the honeymoon period and it is excitement all around. Like in love, and in marriage. In jobs, too. The world seen through rose-tinted glasses of fascination. Tints that dissipate. Fascinations that fade. Promises to last a lifetime that do not even last longer than an orgasm. That premature disenchantment. Is there a love where the fascination never wanes? Is there a job where the excitement never dies? Is there any human pursuit where the marginal utility never diminishes? Meh wonders.

The chief motivator and mentor (CMM) was in charge of the MT programme. It was the first year of its introduction in India, an experiment trying to recreate its success in other countries. He notices the indifference of some, including Mehraz's. He then motions to the ever-obliging assistant manager, Giri Chamcha: 'Play *the* video.' (Chamcha did, obligingly, and smiled in acceptance of a gratitude that was never offered to him.

Tiny tyrants. Psyched sycophants.) 'This one is sure to get everyone excited. It will get your hearts beating and blood pumping; like …'

Kandhon se milte hain kandhe

Kadmon se kadam milte hain

Con Ass *waale chalte hain jab aise tho*

Dil dushman ke hilte hain …

Substandard parody of a high-octane Bollywood song that has soldiers under training gets played, with name of the company thrown in lavishly in between.

Bombing sequences … War cries … Killing … Chest thumping …

Applause again. Lights back on. Faces that were glowing with pride and enthusiasm even without the lights. Meh was seen looking around for the evening's *chaai pakoda*. Today, I should be able to identify onion *pakodas* by the look of it and pick onion *pakodas* alone. How many will I get right today? Meh wondered.

There was one final trick up the CMM's sleeve, for ones like Meh. He had seen many like Meh during his long, depressing career. The final trick that clinches the deal each time.

Lights off. [View>Full screen; Screen brightness>Max]

A projector zoom lever turned this way, then that way.

On a white screen that looked empty and serene until then, suddenly flashed a picture of the ever-smiling CEO, Paddy Lax Man (U.S. transl. for Padmanabhan Lakshmanan), posing right on top of the ladder of corporate success while taking great pains to balance himself on top with all the accumulated flab. The poster boy for success in insurance industry the world over. That too an Indian.

'Dear MT friends, it gives me immense joy to share with you that twenty-five years ago, Paddy was sitting in the same seats as you all are sitting now. Well ... not exactly the same seat, and not really here, but in the U.S. But the same MT orientation, you see. Ha! Ha! Ha! In each of you, I see a Paddy and the future of Con Ass, and I am certain it is in safe hands. I wish you all success. Your posting details will be shared with you shortly.'

This finally brought some glow even to Mehraz's dark face. He loves pretending to be dark for the world.

There is hope. It needn't be sales as feared. I will get to work in multiple corporate functions. The more respectable marketing, the cerebral actuarial and investment divisions, the glamorous institutional business and then finally, like Paddy, right at the helm! A hopeful Meh mused.

The glow was short-lived. Blame it on the man's short-sightedness. A certified, chronic myopic whose limited views on things could never be fully corrected, even with thick glasses. Everyone was handed over their appointment letters. Meh's summarised, read as follows: 'Selling of Con Ass individual insurance policies through our new Corporate Agency distribution partner in Kerala, Mammon Stock Brokers Limited (MBL), Kottayam branch.' A match made in hell.

… And with a magical swoosh—while most of his college friends were set to extend their hostel life of fun and frolic in the big cities—Meh got teleported into the land of Latex, Letters, and Lakes.

Of left-behinds. Also of no life. And of no lights.

On a hartal day.

THE RED-LETTER DAY

Comrade Red Hat Senior was in charge of the party in the state. But the party was in power only in one state. That made Red Hat Sr the de facto in-charge for the country, its most powerful. He celebrates success at the party headquarters drinking spurious, insipid Russian vodka and slurping on cheap Chinese noodles certified unfit for human consumption in the mainland. Rejected and dumped. Received with thanks.

For a railway station that gets very few arrival passengers, there were many seen stranded in the portico that day, with no further means of conveyance. That is how it works on hartal days. Trains and flights are spared, not the ones who want to make it into or out of them. The more people get stranded, the more successful the hartal. Newspapers have to carry it on the front page: 'Life has come to a standstill.' Anything less than *standstill* is a failure. And Red Hat Sr has made it a habit to win, at least here. Among those stranded were foreigners who had come from as far as South America and eastern Europe, made it past Russia and China, and finally got tripped up by a tiny communist state down south in India. Most were headed for Kumarakom, a favourite tourist destination. Then there were some local pilgrims, patients to a medical college and some interstate travellers. And a man on his first day to work.

Gandhi had championed it. Miffed, the British left. Gandhi died, hartal died. Everywhere else, except here. All political parties compete to celebrate these disruptions—the red the green the saffron the white; the left the right the middle; then the wing-less the stand-less the colourless—like a local festival, and no one wants to miss out. Taxis and rickshaws do not ply. Those who do will have to be paid a bomb, only to be vandalised soon. Bombed or stoned. Windshields, foreheads broken. There was a hartal when Saddam Hussein was assassinated by a 'capitalist, imperialist America.' Saddam was a revolutionary running a peaceful dictator state. Red Hat Sr loved them all; revolutionaries, dictators, tyrants. He had their red-garlanded pictures in his office, next to red-stained human skulls—a headhunter's prized collectibles. *America* remains a unifying antagonist here, unifying enemies by being the enemies' common enemy!

The shops were all shut on that day too. No vehicles, no food. Only standstill, only hardships. A travel-weary Mehraz stepped outside the portico into bright welcoming sunshine; stretched himself, yawned. A helpless stray dog joined in the pandiculation, letting out a whimper in meek dog-protest on being denied its breakfast of restaurant leftovers. A few angry curs, *barking loudly at all that they did not understand,* joined a group of sloganeers shouting at things they did not understand, too. 'Down, down capitalism'; 'Privatisation *moordabad*'; 'Down with IMF' ... 'Woof, woof! Bow-wow!' ... A symphony of protests. Shouting in *Communese*, barking in *Caninese*. Loyal canines, disloyal masters.

Like every Keralite who knows the rules of the game, Mehraz was prepared. He counted his cigarettes: Six. The hotel is about five kilometres from the station. It is a good thing that this town gets over in five kilometres. That is enough kilometres and cigarettes to smoke out one's frustration. Meh started walking. Through deserted roads lined with larger-than-life paper cut-outs of smiling politicians, fluttering flags and pennants of all possible shades. Those who did not come prepared with cigarettes remained stranded. Remained waiting, for the hartal to get over. Remained hoping, for there to be no fresh hartals in tow. The sudden call for standstill with no prior notice: lightning strikes, as they are called. The only place where *lightning strikes* more than once. Every other day. Almost.

'You are being posted in a state we have categorised alongside J&K in political sensitivity.' The HR had warned him. *Colour-coded* RED! That made sense. There are unions and associations here for private insurance and bank employees, software professionals and film stars, along with hairdressers, toddy-tappers, pensioners, train commuters and just about everyone. An old joke goes that there was once a union formed by those without one and there once was a hartal to protest against unnecessary hartals. The collective brannigan. That legitimised anarchy. Dhows. Trucks. Despair.

They opposed everything, including tractors, computers, ports, airports and the Aadhaar card. It was CIA's plan to steal their biometric information, the party claimed; the same CIA that the party often blames for its election losses, too. Many loyal cadres stood in Aadhaar enrolment queues with eyes firmly shut and hands at the back, fingers intertwined, unwilling to part with their biometrics. Blind and crippled. They shooed many a corporate away, Indian and foreign, including John Hopkins that had plans of setting up a large hospital here. Then the comrades went in hordes to the U.S. for treatment. Including to Hopkins. Including Red Hat Sr. They then traded their doctrines and dhotis for ill-fitting suits and *bandhgalas*. Attempting to look like diplomats, they appeared like hypocrites. Eschewed dialectics, espoused materialism. The cadre still cheered. *Inquilab Zindabad!*

The final cigarette. Out goes the smoke in perfect rings. One, one and a half …

Mehraz was also left-leaning once, like his father. Like most children of most fathers. For most people, religion and politics remain sheer inheritances, spreading through blood and genes. Like a genetic disorder. No application of free mind, or of free will. They mindlessly inherit and believe theirs to be the best without ever attempting to know what they reject and revile. Many end up loving their parents' religion more than they love their parents. Some shun their parents' values, abandon parents even, but never the parents' religion. Never such unquestioning trust of a fellow human's words otherwise. Not totally so when it is of a mystical man's revelations, of another's second coming or of incarnations. Or about the superiority of one over another; still worse, about only one of them being true. They ask no questions, demand no proofs, seek no experiences. Then they spill blood and actively spread it through blood; others' and theirs.

Extremism of any kind is a problem, religious and political. Both right-wing fascism and left-wing fanaticism are equally worrisome. They are both mirror images of the same ugly truth. What is on the left of one is on the right of the other. That's it. For now.

Communism was once the intellectual's solution to the problems of the working class. Ones who do not even break a sweat attempting to wipe the tears of those who do. Those problems do not exist today; intellectuals, too. Yet they want the cadre to believe both still do. With non-existent problems and outdated solutions, and with no one capable of or allowed to bring it in sync with the times, they struggle for relevance, the world over. They believe that starting with the Industrial Revolution, every economic activity has led to exploitation and inequality that need to be eradicated. Since we can't eradicate exploitation, we eradicate economic activity. Since we can't establish utopian egalitarianism by making the poor rich, we make the rich poor. Simple solutions. A happy cadre.

Ignorance that is the opium of the masses. Spectres that still hang around and haunt ...

The cigarette and the thoughts died down as Meh reached a hotel that had its shutters downed to protect the glass windows in front. He was sneaked in through the back door past a kitchen that was shut as workers could not make it. 'No wages for the (proletarian) workers today, Sir. No breakfast for (the bourgeois) you today, Sir. Only *machine tea*, for you. Only hardships, for everyone.' That is not even tea. Meh declined.

A five-kilometre-long walk on the first day of work. Lugging heavy baggage and thoughts. An already tired, frustrated young man was getting ready to go to work. To be the newest employee of a capitalistic corporate in a communist state.

Another contemptible petty bourgeois in the making.

... Is there a man more lost than the one forced to walk the cobbled path of conformity?

ANOTHER FORCED BAPTISM; NO CRIES

The Continental office was about half-an-hour's walk from the hotel. *Nah!* That just won't suffice. Red Hat Sr always needs more details about common man's life coming to a standstill to be happy. He will be happy to know that it is a standstill for Mehraz after a long walk. He will be happier to know that Mehraz will have to now walk back on the same road that he had just walked, lugging all the baggage and thoughts.

Walk right back, all the way, Mehraz. Okay, no more exaggerations—half of the way. But, still …

9:58 a.m. An irate, empty-stomached man ran inside an air-conditioned office, perspiring. Tie, a black bag and everything. Sweaty patches on a brand-new shirt. Continental Assurance India Private Limited. A board read, right above shutters that were half shut. In fear or in anticipation of the moment the *hartalers* would descend, hurl some abuse and stones, break a few glasses and the shutters would be fully downed. One more office shut. Economic activity *stand-stilled*. Capitalism thwarted. Revolution triumphed. *Inquilab Zindabad!* Long live the revolution.

This is the office of the Individual Agency Division. A different division that recruits individuals as part-time agents who earn a commission for torturing, luring or emotionally blackmailing their friends and relatives into buying Continental's policies. There were three MTs in that division trying to get policies from their relatives. Meh met them all. He does not have a seat here. He has to be at the MBL office from the next day. MBL is the Corporate Agent for selling Continental's insurance products and earns corporate commissions as intermediary fees. Meh has to source policies from MBL clients, not from his relatives. That was the only minor difference. A major relief, too.

Meh was offered instant tea from the office vending machine and was introduced to one of the senior sales managers who was to spend a day prepping him for a lifetime of sales. Meh declined the fake tea, again. (*Toldya* already. Take it away.) The man's services, he could not. Another paunchy man, he was still hungover from a night of excessive drinking. He had recently enrolled for a Hindi-speaking course in an attempt to impress his boss in Mumbai and would pepper his speech with Hindi phrases totally unnecessarily.

Another Forced Baptism; No Cries

The prep got underway. First: Telesales.

To solicit business over an unsolicited call—*Insurance is the subject matter of solicitation*. The first mandatory, nugatory disclaimer that an undeveloped Regulator insists on; funny too. To build relationship with that grumpy man on the other side. To catch him at that exact wrong moment when he was doing something very important. Or about to. Never when he is waiting for this one call. No one ever does, you see.

'*Achaa*, start with greetings.'

'I'm sorry, what?'

'Greetings. You have to start by greeting, Mehraz.'

'Ah! That one, sure.'

'All good relationships begin with a phone call, *betaa*.' Ugly grin. 'Do this right and you can hear a smile over the phone.' The salesman turned poetic. 'Then, you introduce our company in a few words and seek an appointment. *Sim Ble*. Here is the telemarketing script. Try *karlo*.'

A man hesitant to call even his father, much less greet him or unnecessarily ask him how he is feeling that morning or on any morning for that matter, here he is, Mehraz, about to check with a random man about his feelings, and still worse, solicit his interest. He picked up the receiver hoping the line wouldn't connect. Perhaps the *hartalers* had set on fire the telephone exchange or even the rest of the town. He skipped dialling the last digit, a ploy that did not work the second time. The sales manager has seen it all.

'*Karo, karo*. Go ahead, do it.' Like an accomplished sinner encouraging the undefiled to do it right the first time, he was full of wicked enthusiasm.

'Hel-llo … He-ello …' Trembling voice from a choked throat relayed smoothly over cables to Mr Grumpy at the other end.

'*Aara?*' [Who's it?]

'Very good morning, Sir.' (You say that when you have to sound 'very' courteous. *Phoney* etiquettes.)

'*Aaraada uvve?*' [Who's it? With disgust.]

'How are you doing today morning, Sir?' (Greetings done.)

'*Oh! ennaa parayaanaanne, maduppiraanenne.*' [Oh! What to say, it is all dull and gloom.]

This, Meh was to realise, was the standard response by everyone in that town: '*Oh! maduppiraanenne.*' The guy could be the priest at the local parish or the local Member of Parliament, a baker, a banker, a planter, a professor, a preacher; anyone. They all say this: *maduppiraanenne*. Perhaps this is why most religions have a standard greet-and-response template. Can't imagine one saying *Praise be to the creator* and a response that says *Oh maduppiraanenne.* They negate all things blasphemous, or brilliant, at the outset itself. Exordiums. Invocations. Initiations. Proselytised at birth. Congenitally crippled. *Void ab initio.*

'Sir, this is Mehraz, calling from Continental Assurance. If you could allow a few minutes to introduce our company and its value proposition to you.'

'Oh! Raavile thanne udayippamayittu irangiyekkuvaa alliyo. Vachechum poyineda. Manushyane menakkeduthaan …'

This is pretty much the standard response everywhere, not just here, and mildly translates to, 'Out to con people right in the morning itself. Hang up, will you?'

Hang on a minute, but the script says, 'Sure, go ahead. I would love to hear more. Thank you for having called.' Do they really say this anywhere? Other than in sales scripts? In the consumerist U.S.? Meh wondered.

The response definitely was not part of the script that Meh had. Nothing was as per a script Meh wished he had. Everything is scripted in a way he wished it never was, and all he could do was act some uncomfortable acts. Like a helpless actor playing the saddest role someone else wrote. A sad play of lonely and confused characters.

Half written by an unknown author that the characters have no access to. Yet they keep playing, unaware of and anxious about how it ends. He plays. He acts. He bides his time as the story evolves.

Meh disconnected the call and looked at the manager.

'*Achaa*, introvert? No problem. Extrovert *ban jaa*. Be an extrovert.'

What? How?

Then, a long lecture on what went wrong and what could have been better. Longer lecture on the problems with 'these newbies'—that universal condescension of the accomplished, as if they all started out with experience. A much longer lecture on his own accomplishments as a sales manager. Appraisals and judging that start from day one.

'Could you show me once how it is done?'

'Sure, sure; dial any number.'

Meh dialled the same number and handed over the phone.

'Didn't I just tell you b@$**** not to call me again? A disguised voice and you think I don't …' The sales manager abruptly hung up.

There were no smiles heard over the phone as promised. But the swear words reverberated across the whole

Another Forced Baptism; No Cries

office and no one reacted as though anything unusual happened.

'Do you smoke, Mehraz? Come, let us take a break.'

It was more sales philosophy all the way down to the smoking corner and back. Meh felt he just smoked his longest cigarette ever. A lot of advice on how to appear good even if you are not good. How to show a keen interest even when you couldn't care less. How to fake sympathy, admiration, servitude. To be congenial. To be cordial. To concur. Never to confront. Never to share your views if they conflict with others'. Never to speak your mind. To please them all. To do whatever it takes to win that cheque: the single target to be kept in mind. One that will take you closer to your sales targets. *All about targets, dear.*

He turned around in his charioteer seat, egging a circumspect young warrior to action: 'The target justifies the means, Mehraz.' A sales halo appeared and disappeared over the man's head.

He then slowly whispered that sacred mantra in Meh's ears: 'Customer is the king. Customer is always right.'

'Is he?' 'Can he be?'

'Replace customer with boss and you have your answer, Mehraz. Even if it is someone who is your boss for a day.'

Then there was a role play. Of a client meeting, of course. Meh was to try and sell an insurance policy to the sales manager. If there is anything that is worse than an actual client meeting, it is the role play of a client meeting. No man is ever known to have really *sold* anything or achieved any *real* pleasure through role plays, you know right? A *buyer* with no real intention to *buy*, always ready to put down whatever the *seller* has to say, it is a cruel indulgence. (Indulgence for the buyer, cruel for the seller. One that needs to be banned by law in all training sessions; like slavery, like deer hunting.) If the roles were reversed, the other one would also always come a cropper, Meh was certain. But those scripts and the roles we play … Meh knew he had to act this out too. As expected and as if designed, Mehraz failed.

A longer lecture this time. On body language, eye contact, hands in pocket, hands on the lap, legs crossed, legs uncrossed, sympathy, empathy, probing, closure techniques. Meh looked at his watch hoping it is lunchtime or that the *hartalers* would come. Then wondered if he himself should call them here.

'Meh, you see, the problem is, you think you are a sheep and the customer is a lion. Don't you? You are the lion, Mehraz. You are the lion.' A firm hold on his shoulders. A few firm shakes. As if he was shaking in all the leonine spirit into a sheepish Meh.

These are all common stories you see recurring in every sales training. They all buy the same cheap motivational books from the same store, on a sale: Sell Like a Lion, Selling for Dummies, How to Sell Dummies. Only thing that gets sold based on these books are these books alone. Anyone who tells you he can sell anything to anyone is lying. And that thing about *Sell me the Pen*—you just can't do it, unless the person has the need for a pen or to make you look good. All that is substandard sales literature written by people who could never sell. (Yes, that is what they end up doing, mostly—books and literature. Substandard, mostly. I know.) And selling ice cream to Eskimo, you ask? God! He does not need it at all. That is why he is an Eskimo. If he needs one, he will call you. Go sell it to that Bedouin. The real skill is in knowing whom not to sell to. And in not wasting other people's time. Yours too. Don't get fancy always. Salesmanship is not showmanship …

A thunderous voice derails the train of thoughts.

'Be a man, kid. Man up. Strap on a pair.' Teeth grinding. Nostrils flaring. Fists clenching. Belly protruding. 'Become a man! Become a sales manager! … Did you see that? There is a man in sales manager. Isn't that cool? Be that man.'

(There is a *man* even in HR Manager, in fact in every Manager. It is there in Woman, and Mango too. What is your point?)

'You should know this and say it out loud: I AM A LIONNNNNNNN.' The man roared. *BURP!* A whisky-flavoured belch.

'Sure, you are a lion.'

'*Abbey*, not me. *Tu*. You are the lion in this case. Let's try that again. Just repeat after me. I am a lion! I am a lion!'

Meh looked around to see if there was a window he could jump off from. Or to push out this lion with the tummy of a buffalo. Defenestrate the defiler.

'I ... am a lion. I am a ... lion.' (And I just want to run away.) Meh bleated.

'*Shaabaash,* Meh. *Sher hain tu*. Come on, champ! There are biryani packets in the pantry. Take only one, okay? We meet after lunch.'

Meh ran out for a smoke and some fresh air.

The pantry was beside a small training hall. A new batch of agents was having their induction. A smaller version of what Meh had at the swanky hotel near the corporate office in Mumbai.

'Dear Agent friends, it gives me immense joy to share with you that twenty-five years ago, Paddy was sitting in the same seats as you all are sitting now. Well ... not exactly the same seat, and not really here, but in the U.S. But the same Agent orientation, you see. Ha! Ha! Ha! In each of you, I see a Paddy and the future of Con Ass, and I am certain it is in safe hands. I wish you all success.'

That sounded familiar. Heard that before, almost verbatim. Including the *Ha-Ha-Ha* in between. Meh understood the moral of the story—a story with no morals.

At that exact moment, Mehraz was unwillingly baptised into the world of sales. But he did not cry, like how all babies do when baptised. An attempted protest: against doing something without their permission, against being forced into a tattered hand-me-down that they can never outgrow. Meh had stopped protesting of any kind long ago, like everyone else. Never cried other than on his first day at kindergarten and his day of circumcision. Both painful, and forced. (The School: A place helmed by a *demoness* on deputation, *Kunthrandi Rakshasi*, she had retractable fingernails that were red from clawed bottoms and wrenched ears of little children—marks of slavishness on tender hearts forever. A place where all the writing lines and 'impositions' started and his leisure began to be timed as per a table that permitted it only for thirty minutes on every Thursday, and gradually, leisure stopped being a part of his timetables. The Forced Snipping: An undying shame and pain that still lingers—marks of conformity on the gullible that serve as forever-reminders.) Sometimes, he wished he had not stopped crying. At least a muted cry of dissent, before all his slavish abidance and puppetry.

Birth to death. Prenatal to postmortem. Christening to death rituals. Everything in between. Religion, politics, schools, uniforms, education, careers, ethics, propriety, spouse, loans, vacations, waking up, lunch breaks, teatime … Do impositions never end? When does a man ever start making his own choices? When does he stop living others' stories and start living his dreams? When does he start noticing the fetters that get wrought? *Salvation. Moksha. Jannat.* Rewards not available for the free man? Never for the not-dead-yet? Can no man be liberated even while alive? Born or made? Nature or nurture? Free will, anyone? Choose it, be prepared to lose paradise. The *fallen* man. The sinner.

Someone's phone rang in the background.

Sab gandha hain par dhandha hain yeh …

Ek baar fass gayaa toh; tu fass gayaa samajhle.

Khallas!

Meh really wished the protesters descended now and burned the whole place along with him. He was *also* feeling communist and suicidal.

The hartal was a grand success that day.

Vodka and noodles.

THE SALES FAILURES

*T*he next morning Meh was at MBL office. He introduced himself to Shibu as the on-site resource responsible for cross-selling Continental's products to MBL clients. Shibu knew. There was a mail that had heralded his arrival: a bright-starred one, as labelled in Shibu's inbox.

Mammon Brokers is a stock broker preferred by the elderly who view day trading as their day job. All of them make friends here, a few make profits and most make losses. Yet, something brings them back every morning at nine. They spend an entire day drinking free sugarless black teas; yelling at times, going totally silent at other times. They share their hopes, fears and lunches with the stock dealers. The dealers, in turn, give *all* of them *exclusive* tips on which shares to bet on. (Psst! Only for you.) Second-guessing a whimsical market's absurd swings and violent oscillations. A crazy free fall at times like a suicidal skydiver with no parachute, sending many a hyperventilating man's hopes, net worth and blood pressure into a frenzied spiral; or irrationally beefed up at other times, as if on steroids. Analysts—far worse than crooked astrologers, slightly better than weather forecasters—incapable of predicting even an enraged wife's next move, delivering prophecies: *technically* flawed, *fundamentally* useless. Amidst all this chaos, these day traders do what is called short-selling: a sort of gamble in the hope that they can make a quick fortune. They are the ones who hope for a jackpot that never happens. Then they come back the next day hoping for a jackpot which never happens, too. It continues ...

People like Shibu needed these day traders because their constant buying and selling meant brokerage income. The investors, on the other hand, hold their shares for long and would barely sell. They give no brokerage, the regular revenue that these broking houses need. Shibu was not sure where to fit insurance into this. The number of heartbreaks these old men suffered on a daily basis, Meh felt insurance would fit in just right. Shibu had concerns about troubling his clients and losing brokerage in the process. He was also suspicious of the investment products Con Ass had. But the high commissions insurance companies offer are always enticing for the distributors. So, caught between brokerage and commission, budget pressures and client relations, Shibu was a torn man.

'Listen, I will not be able to sell or even push my clients. I can, at best, suggest to a few people I am close to. The dealers will also help you with leads. But you may ... no ... you should get yourself introduced to all clients and do your thing. I just want sales to happen. We sure could use some commission income; plus, there is a lot of buzz around this even with my management. But remember, it is primarily your baby.' Shibu was quick to establish the paternity of an illegitimate, unwanted child.

Almost three months passed. No sales. Only buzz. Pressure was mounting on Shibu. On Meh, too. Shibu was due for retirement in a few months; an old man still anxious about his future, bitter about his past. A few extra bucks, some appreciatory mails and certificates would give him something to feel good about. But nothing happened. Mehraz was a failure already. And he has not even gotten started.

Then came the Christmas season. With Christmas came a lot of faith and hope.

'Israelin naadhanayi vaazhum eka daivam ...'

A popular devotional song in praise of the unitary God of Israel—one of the *many* unitary gods there are—reverberates across town during that time. Mobile ringtones, car reverse alarms, loudspeakers ...

With Christmas also came the non-residents (NRIs: non-resident Indians as they are called) like Santa.

With them came a lot of money and some happiness.

Lonely parents got their annual share of love, and insurers, their premium. Sons and daughters, husbands and wives got their annual share of parental and spousal affection respectively. It is a happy time in that town, the only one. Shibu was happy, like every branch manager. They will all be lining up at NRI houses with cheap plum cakes; at rich NRI houses, with rich plum cakes—less cheap at least. Shibu would specially wear his cheap red tie for them. Richness and cheapness commingle in joyous spirit during this festive season. Along with hoarded-up family love, stashed monies in non-resident bank accounts also come out during this time (all the money from legalised human trade that keeps a state with industry-free zones very *rich*). Then, everyone and everything goes back and remains dormant for one year. Then, they wait for the next Christmas—sons and daughters, wives and husbands, fathers and mothers; every salesman, too. For renewal of love and investments. Only for one they would get timely reminders. Only one everyone takes special care not to lapse.

They call this land the Empty Nest, too. No 'L' for this one. Okay, *Lonely Nest* would work.

Houses waiting for people; a town, too. A childless, *barren* town with unoccupied palatial houses built by men who live in cubbyholes in rich countries. Too many of them that a government had proposed additional tax on these locked-up houses. Now they are busy converting empty government schools into retirement homes. Houses so desolate, some are bereft of shadows, even. Some of them house a widowed mother or father. Sometimes waiting to be widowed; wondering who is the lucky one to escape first, worried who will be the one to be left behind. A sad game of musical wheelchairs and deathbeds. Death: the only thing in life to look forward to, the only visitor to a forlorn house. Then, a trail of pointless visitors to a house with no host—to meet lifeless bodies and meaningless propriety norms; to display affection and wreaths emblazoned with names of the affected; to offer hugs and respects that will never be returned. If only these visitors do not wait for death to initiate …

Of all Meh's failed attempts at sales, a few stand out. First was during that Christmas season. The prospect was a rich NRI, of course. He was one of Shibu's biggest clients. He screamed affluence and *NRIness* from every part of his existence. A big burly man with a wicked grin, he smelled of alcohol and perfume, cigarette and meanness. A man of many vices including a needless use of English that he believed made him elite. At least in Kottayam. A man who takes great care to keep his children from learning any Indian language so that they can be elite, even in Bradford. *Eliter,* in Kottayam. Elite brown little Englishmen, like dolls with faulty parts, speaking strange tongues. A man who takes great pride in seeing his parents struggle to converse in English with their grandchildren. *Elitest*, in Kottayam.

Suku, his name. A *Suu*, a *Kuuu*. S. K. Tom as he preferred to be called. [U.K. transl. for Suku Thommichan]

Like all his friends, Suku had tried doing some software courses, and failed. Then, like most of them, he won over a compassionate (rich) nurse from Kottayam and turned the (rich) NRI husband of an (rich) NRI wife. He now runs an Indian restaurant overstaffed with underpaid illegal immigrants in Bradford, U.K. Every night after work, they all slipped into secret underground chambers, uncounted and unaccounted, like cockroaches. A rich man's success story. A slow but steady growth, from his formative years in Kottayam to Yorkshire, like of a snail. From a baby snail to a full-grown one by the time it crawled across the border of one land lot to another. A slithery snail. A slimy trail. Unread—— Unmeant—— Unsigned—— Oh! Forget all that. None of these really matter. No one here asks a venerated non-resident what his job is. All he has to say is *'Yenn Naarr Raiyy.'* No more questions asked. As if it is a full-time job, a highly respectable one.

'I can't seem to get my head around this, Shibu. Why don't you put together a slide deck that summarises this at a *high level?* With some neat bulleted points. Maybe throw in a simulation that projects the likely growth? On a million rupees annual investment!' Suku sounded just like every Indian dude who does this software stuff, or ever tried doing.

'A what, Sir?' Shibu understood nothing other than the million rupees. That too after a bit of mental math in a totally blanked-out head converting million to lakhs.

'Some sort of presentation, Shibu. And some real numbers.'

'Oh! *Pee Pee Tee*. That this kid will do, Sir. He is *Yem Bee Yay* and all. He is an MT.' (Shibu always had an uncanny way of making MT sound more like *empty* than *MT*! Meh suspected.)

'Cool, that works. So you get it, right? Mail it to me at hotmale_skt27@hotmail.com and we take it forward. I don't have much time, let's close this out soon, man. All right?'

Meh nodded. Like a kid.

A million rupees! That was almost the annual budget of an MT those days.

A million rupees! That is almost what it takes for a branch manager to retire with pride, even today.

Merry Xmas. Santa is here.

'Meh, you start making the PPT and yeah, give him the *stimulation* or whatever it is that he asks for. Anything Meh, I just want you to keep that man happy. If he is pleased, you will be the star. And you finally get to use that *entheppenadi* that you *chumma* carry otherwise. Happy?'

Entheppenadi: Shibu's very own word for the personal laptop that Meh never had any real reason to carry around, until now. (Of course, other than for everything that every lonely young man his age is *prone* to use a laptop for.) Thingamajig will be the closest. Thingamajig said with a lot of scorn. *Chumma* is something my people *chumma* say, just like that. For no reason. *Chumma!* [Summa. Sumne. Yunhi.]

All that the company had given Meh were some brochures and a blue-coloured book that had the premium tables. Digital and online support systems were still in their early stages. This is what happens to people during transition phases—that intervening period, that in-between limbo. You still have only the old; there is already a need for the new; you don't know what to do. Meh checked around.

'*Da*, we don't use all this. We just request for money and they give, sometimes. I have seen trainers use some PPTs. But simulation and all? …' Sandy, the MT from Individual Agency Division, was helpless.

The Sales Failures

Meh—unhelped, unskilled—set out to invent the wheel himself. Precious time lost. Shibu was busy tending to other NRIs, with renewed vigour. Occasional reminders came to Meh. Finally, Meh got enough material to piece together something, but he was mindful of time already lost. So he devised a plan:

Meh would call up Suku and tell him he has already mailed the files and check if he received it. When Suku says he hasn't, Meh can blame it on the file size or the ISPs or the mailer *daemon* or whatever that is; anything other than his ineptitude. Then, he would seek time until end of the day to *resend* it. With an apology, of course. Suku receives the mail, feels impressed—a million rupees in the bargain. A happy Shibu. A happy Meh.

The baptised salesman was attempting to write his own stories now, minus the morals. And this one deal would mean the ideal start to his sales career. Sales, after all, is not that difficult.

Meh took out his phone.

Dialling: *Suku-India Num* …

'Yeah, the guy from MBL. Tell me, dude.'

'Yes, Sir. I had mailed you last week and was wondering if you had a chance to go through the files.'

'Oh yes, man ... I DID!!!! I forwarded it to my chartered accountant too. He is okay with it, largely; just a few basic queries. Let's close it out in a day or two. I will swing by your office sometime. Tell Shibu, too. Cheque is fine, right? Alrighty then. And yeah ... Merry Xmas, man.'

A fibbing pawn stymied by a burly lying king! In a treacherous game—of powerless pawns and powerful kings, of wily snakes and no ladders.

Here, a prospect who received a mail that was not even typed. A mail that was forwarded that was not even sent. A chartered accountant who okayed a proposal that was not even prepared. A promise that will never be honoured. A cheque that will never be signed. A merry Xmas that someone never meant. A commitment that Meh made to his Continental bosses that will never be fulfilled. A branch manager about to retire, but with no dignity. A domino of lies ...

Do all these make Meh a colossal liar? A collateral one, at least? It was Meh's first time learning that it is not just sales people who lie. Even buyers do. A buyer who so slyly disowns, and distances from, his own words.

A deceitful ventriloquist. A voiceless doll. A stringless puppet.

The target loomed larger than before. Embarrassments, humiliations, insults. All set to intensify every Friday evening. The downstream impact was unnerving. Sales, after all, is not that easy.

That night the darkness grew darker than usual. It was the night they reintroduced load-shedding: the daily planned power outage of thirty minutes. They do it every time the monsoons fail, or when they feel there isn't enough water in the reservoirs or enough darkness in that town. From the pushcarts to the five-star hotels of Kumarakom, everyone now has candlelit dinners: the haves the have-nots; the whites the darks the greys; the non-residents the expatriates the homeless. A fair socialist distribution of darkness. Candles, lanterns; cigarettes, *bidis* …

Ambassador beckoned. Meh showered.

A flight to Heathrow carried a burly man from Nedumbasseri airport after a few days. An unsigned cheque; the smells, too. A wicked grin flashed in the evening sky.

Merry Xmas, everyone!

SALES FAILURES CONTINUED

The new year saw Shibu turn into a more resentful man, a man whose Christmas was spoiled by an Insurance Grinch. He had always believed that any salesman in Kottayam who failed during Christmas is doomed to fail for the rest of the year, likely for the rest of his life. He felt it was all because Meh did not handle Suku properly. Not stimulated enough, perhaps? He made some snide remarks and felt better. Like a donkey that brays to get over its lust. That man happy blaming the other for losses; that man never as upset as he pretends to be; that man who always finds his joys in making others feel guilty. A reason to blame, a reason to be happy.

'*Ketto Miniye, nammude officelum undu nokkukooli vaangunnavar. Vallya kooliyaa. Nammude Kanyakan.*' [You know what, Mini? Even in our office there are people who get *nokkukooli*, a hefty one. Our *Kanyakan*.]

Sales Failures Continued

All of Shibu's revulsion was evident in that one remark to Mini. Towards someone who does no business. Towards someone who was paid an 'unjustly high' salary. Not sure which of the two was always the bigger problem for Shibu. Towards the *Kanyakan*: the 'He-Virgin,' as Shibu liked to call a novice Mehraz. Shibu's contribution to the lexicon of a land that never bothered to give male virginity a thought, or a word, until then.

(*Nokkukooli:* The wages you pay someone for looking at others do the work, literally. Not for overseeing. Let me explain. You may engage any worker of your choice at whatever wage you want to pay them. But the trade unions here have a right to their wages that they arbitrarily decide, whether you employ one of them or not. Work is optional; wages, a matter of right. They stand by the side and look at your workers loading and unloading stuff, but they still have to be paid their wage in the end. It is called ransom or extortion elsewhere; here, it is legitimate wage. Again, something that the courts have banned, on paper. Like the many things the courts have banned, yet remain legitimate in practice. Something that Meh could never get any of his friends from outside Kerala to believe. They know that Meh is delusional; his *state*, too delusional.)

Meh knew he should feel insulted at Shibu's snub. He was about to; he then felt it was funny. Shibu does have a sense of humour. That has to be his second-best joke. He himself was the first. Meh smiled, like a clown—a clown with a painted smile, behind which could be a weeping man. But the painted upward arch of the clown's lips, a permanent fixture, gives the impression that the man is always happy. Meh also carried about an arch those days.

And Meh continued to fail in his sales attempts. Well, the next attempt was not really a failure. Even today, Meh does not count it as one. No. At least today, Meh does not count it as one. Yes, that reads better.

The prospect was *Appachan*. *Appachan* can be a chosen name, an alias or surname in these parts. It can also refer to a grandfather, father or any elderly man. This all-rolled-into-one multipurpose *Appachan* was about seventy. He had spent a good part of his life running a canteen at one of the steel factories in the North. Now he has come back for good planning to spend his retired life tending to his ancestral fields and to the meagre equity investments he holds with MBL. He also hopes for some regular income from a pension plan he wished to purchase from the perceivably safer Government Insurance Corporation (GIC). Shibu got wind of it and has since been pressuring Mini *Chechi* and Meh to convince *Appachan* to go with Continental instead.

Mini, the elderly lady in office, was semi-sympathetic to Meh. She was guarded in her sympathy, for she knew one should never be too sympathetic to an insurance salesman, especially a struggling one. She also shared the common fear that forcing clients for insurance could spoil her relationships with them. For that reason she referred very few of her clients to Meh though she claimed she always had Meh in her prayers. So if Mini *Chechi* was to be believed, which Meh did, she had made more requests to a certain Nazarene than she did to any man in Kottayam. Something had to work, Meh was hopeful.

Continental did not have an insurance policy that would meet the requirement of *Appachan*: an immediate payment annuity. For most distributors like MBL, the best insurance policy is one that offers them the highest commission, that is, the one that charges the customer the most. Need-based selling only meant one thing in that world: targets and commission needs of the distributor. Okay, two things. (Mistake *Ji*. Human. Forgive.) Even most insurance policies mature in thirty years. Some people, like Shibu, never do.

Shibu was not too hopeful as he knew *Appachan* was risk-averse and could still go with GIC. 'The old man is so stingy and calculating, he takes one cautious step at a time, as if walking a minefield on crutches. Never even smiles, walks around with a pair of dentures in a glass bottle instead!' Shibu prepped Meh as he does before every meeting—yet another prickly prospect. But, it is never easy for most people to say 'No,' especially at seventy. This is where sales people like Shibu and Mehraz find an opportunity. Meh was asked to visit *Appachan* and turn the hesitant *No* into a hesitant *Yes*, at least.

Sandy said he wished to join Meh for the meeting. Life has been particularly hard for Sandy compared to the other two MTs in his division. Son of a retired schoolteacher, he was finding it real tough. The other two raked in easy business and big policies, thanks to their NRI families. There were always appreciatory mails sent and celebratory cakes cut for them. Sandy had to cut a sorry figure in office always, so he was happy to get away. Also, he was keen to see how sales happened with MBL clients.

In the front yard, perched on wooden planks, the two men saw a tyre-less old car in a garage that shared its wall with a room in which *Appachan* sleeps alone. Once an object of great admiration and the centre of family's attention, now left to rot by a timeworn wall—the car, that is. It is not clear where the junk-filled garage ended and where the bedroom started, and to which one the wall, or the man, really belonged. *Ammachi* [fem. noun equivalent for *Appachan,* an old lady; his wife, in this case] sleeps in a room diagonally opposite *Appachan's* at the farthest possible corner, and they would meet halfway at the dining hall, thrice a day, sharing cold meals and stony silences.

Sales Failures Continued

Appachan greeted both men in. They are generally good to visitors here, even to insurance salesmen. Definitely better than how they are over the phone. *Appachan* was quick to get to the topic:

'*Mone* [Son], this is my savings of a lifetime. They were saying it is beneficial if I invest with you all. But somehow, I would be more comfortable giving this money to GIC. My brother-in-law is an agent with them. Mini was saying you are the GIC of America … Is it so?'

'*Ediye, chaaya.*' *Appachan* shouted out to *Ammachi* asking for tea to be served to the visitors. 'Anything else?'

(*A policy, if you may. Ha! Ha! Ha!* Stale jokes were Meh's thing, every salesman's. In an attempt to lighten the mood. It only worsens things.)

'Well, *Appacha*, what she said is correct. We are indeed quite big. And about the product, you anyway invest in equity. You know the risks, especially in the short run, and its rewards too, don't you?'

'Yes, yes. I do. Mini also said it is good for the long term, though she didn't have any details. She said you will explain in detail.'

'Yes, *Appacha*, these are all long-term investments. Ten to fifteen years.' Then, Meh made that long, passionate sales pitch, parrot-fashion. Long term vs. short term, marathon vs. sprint, risk vs. reward, duration and sensitivity, Sharpe ratio and standard deviation, Keynes and Adam Smith, quantitative easing and monetary policy, El Niño and La Niña ... Just about everything no seventy-year-old has a need to know.

Appachan interrupted.

'See, these days, I don't even buy a raw banana in the hope that I will be around when it turns ripe. How can I invest so much money into something to get my returns only after ten–fifteen years?'

'*Chaaya kudikku, Mone.*' [Have tea, son.] Mehraz just got served.

That is one big nasty foul, *Appacha*. Totally off the script. The role play and sales scripts did not have this as a possible objection. Scripts and plays that never match realities. *Appachan* was definitely not playing by the rules of a handbook he never had. They never give it to the prospects, you see. An amateur salesman did not have much of a response to that genuine objection of *Appachan*. He tried staring into eternity, as if his answers were to appear there. There was no eternity ...

Meh saw *Ammachi* monitoring the goings-on, intensely and intently, through the corners of her cataract-dimmed eyes, as if installed for surveillance by her GIC agent brother. Bejewelled heavily in gold like a forgotten bride who sat rooted to a teak chair for aeons. Bright colours of the wedding saree had faded into dull white as the aureate lady sat glittering and shrivelling, staring fiercely at a world that had long ignored her, with deep-seated distrust. On an ebony dining table next to her were tiny ceramic pickle jars and a multiuser denture in a water-filled bottle. Drowning and gasping, bubbles emitting, grinning and mocking. One that a stingy *Appachan* and his wife share whenever they have to bite ruthlessly. A toothless couple taking turns to grin at a tongue-tied salesman. *Appachan*: grinning, mocking. *Ammachi*: mocking, grinning. Then, a final grin. *Blummm!* The final bubble. Then it died, grinning. Meh: still charmless and wordless.

'That is true, *Appacha* ... no, but ...' Meh then tried laughing that awkward laugh they always do when they have nothing to say. He tried hard to keep the fake smile and the cheer on. A dead denture.

'No, but, I trust you, *Mone*.' A generous miser, charitable enough, lent words to a wordless salesman, filling the blanks. 'Even the folks at MBL, I have known them for so long. I will see if I can split the amount and give you some part of it. After all, what are we if we don't trust each other. Isn't it, *Mone*? ... *Chaaya kudichilla;* you haven't finished the tea yet.'

Trust? Yes.

Trust us to take away forty-five percent of your first year's premium. Trust us to use it to fund our glitzy hotel stays, foreign tours and hefty salaries. Then trust us to fleece you a little less the next year onwards. Forty, thirty-five, thirty and so on. Then trust us to give you enough returns so that in the end you get back your capital, at least. Then trust us to give you enough disclaimers to absolve us of all responsibilities in the event the markets act funny and despite our investment expertise, for which you pay another extra fee, trust us to help you end up with less than what you would have if the money was kept under your mattress. Even after factoring in a share for rodents, leeches and termites. We are peskier and pricier. We wear ties, you see. And if in between you need your money back, trust us to charge you a penalty for returning your own money. A penalty steeper than what the worst gold digger would raise as an alimony—Yes, it is all about trust. It is a win-win too. We win. We win again. And there is a lot of give and take as well. You keep giving, we keep taking ...

How do I sell such a dubious proposition to a trusting old man? Meh wondered. He stared into eternity again, hoping for a solution.

Meh's solution shocked *Appachan*. It shocked the gilded *Ammachi*. It shocked Sandy. It shocked Meh, too.

'Well, *Appacha* ... why don't you give the money to GIC!'

Sales Failures Continued

A stunned *Appachan* was suddenly rendered wordless. 'No ... but ... not like that ... I will somehow try to help you ...' He stuttered.

'No, *Appacha*, it is better you invest with one insurer and not split the money. Give it to GIC. Just don't tell Mr Shibu that I told.'

The two men gulped their teas and got up to leave. A relieved, happy man came out all the way to see them off. Or, just to ensure that they were really gone.

Sandy was silent for as long as he could manage not to make eye contact with Meh.

Over a cigarette and tea, Meh caught Sandy's glance. *This isn't how it usually goes.* Meh said without saying.

Sure. Sandy nodded without nodding.

'Good job selling GIC policy to a Continental prospect,' and he burst out laughing.

A laugh they still share about Meh *successfully* selling his first policy, doesn't matter it was for a competitor, every time they catch up over a beer and some memories.

That evening Meh was not sure if he should be laughing or crying.

He does not remember laughing, for sure.

MONDAY AGAIN, BUT WHY?

Not any Monday. The Monday that Shibu had spoken about. That Friday, you remember? A meeting, a red tie, some tea, much humiliation and a plan in mind. The Monday after that Friday. The 'we will start afresh from Monday' Monday. Yeah, that one.

Meh was back in the office early, back from the neighbouring city. On a train. It was full of people. They all looked like how people do inside trains on Monday mornings. Much blue, many Mehs. All getting off at some station or the other, hurrying to jump off even before the train stopped. Mostly onto platforms. That premature evacuation: in aircrafts, trains, buses. Everyone rushing as if they are all determined to reach somewhere on time. Still no one ever reaches anywhere on time anywhere in this country.

Meh was in no hurry, yet he reached office before time that morning. There was an air of anticipation, a sort of premonition. Meh knew something significant was to happen that morning. Some days are like that. You wake up with that sort of feeling, don't you? You know it even before it happens, don't you?

Mini *Chechi* offered Meh a consolatory smile and an assuring nod. She then pointed at the wall and asked him to look there. He saw a lizard with a walrus moustache maul a fly. Wings falling off and all that.

What about it?

'*Poda*. Not that, silly.'

A gold-plated crucifix of a man crucified on a wooden cross. On a Friday. A reminder that crucified men can be resurrected or that a man has to be crucified first to be resurrected later. A reassuring symbol nonetheless. One that venerates crucifixion as much as the resurrection. Wood to gold. Man to god.

Mini *Chechi re-nodded*, in reassurance. Twice. Reassurance to the insurance guy. Taken.

The Pretty One offered a pretty smile. Nothing more. Meh has never heard her speak. She always gave the impression she wanted to say something, but never did. She had a slight squint in one eye and that made her prettier. She always made sure that she acted pretty too. A beautiful mannequin that never spoke.

The dealers were busy setting up clients or setting up trades for clients. Only Das was keenly looking over the monitor to see what Meh was doing. And then to see what the Pretty One was doing.

The smell of perfume. A tummy. Then walked in a Shibu. There was nothing unusual about the way he went about his work. It was sad, that day as well. Meh hoped Shibu forgets about his existence. He always hoped everyone did.

10:33 a.m. [Meh in Shibu's office]

'Listen, Mehraz, it can't run like this for long. You have had your time. You have been given a long rope; such a long rope that if I were you, I would have hanged myself with it … in shame. It is clear you can't do it. I will speak to your Continental folks on this. Maybe you are good at something else, I don't know. You should figure out something for yourself soon. Until then, I will do the selling. On your part, you just take care of the documentation. Or you want me to do that too?'

'No, Sir. I will handle the documentation bit.'

Meh turned around to leave.

'One more thing, stop being so meh about the whole thing. Just bring in some enthusiasm, you know. When I speak to any prospect, you please play along and not keep a face as if you have nothing to do with it. Whatever

I say, your face should reflect it. At least do that much. *Sheri. Poykko.*'

10:41 a.m. [*Paanwala. Sutta. Chutta.*]

Meh was trying to process what Shibu said. He then tried not to process what Shibu said. But it was all beginning to be a bit overwhelming now. There was already some pressure from the team at Continental as well. Not just on Meh, but on the whole batch of MTs. Talks about their collective non-performance, with likely corrective measures being planned. Most of them were non-starters, like Meh and Sandy. It began as coy whispers through the grapevine, like how it always begins. And now, not so hushed anymore. In an office where even the air conditioners circulate rumours; recycling old ones, spewing fresh ones. Silently.

The boss at Continental had always taken a soft stance towards the MTs, sparing them from his dreaded dressing-downs. He was the 'Territory Manager.' A man with a penchant for using the crudest of swear words in the most imaginative of ways, he was known internally as the *Theri Theri* Manager. An intelligent play of words on the Malayalam word *theri,* which means cuss.

But it was all beginning to change, courtesy one woman: Snitchy. Snitchy was the relationship-in-charge handling MBL at the corporate level. The one on whom success of that relationship solely depended on. Failures could always be blamed on others, like in every corporate. She never liked the MTs much—the MTs, the concept of MTs, the very sight of MTs. She believed the 'kids' were paid an awful lot of money for all the work they were not doing. She had a lot of resentment and took no efforts to hide it.

'Boss, these MTs don't amount to much. The regular sales officers can do twice their business at one-third the cost and half the fuss. Others have also been telling me the same. I am not worried about anything else, but I want MBL to deliver, no matter what. The NRI *belt* around Kottayam is the most critical piece. But that fellow in Kottayam, he is too bookish and meh. Not the *saleoo* type, you know, the kind not cut out for sales. Something needs to be done.'

She filled the boss's ears, mostly about that guy in Kottayam whom she never liked much, sort of. But that was not enough to move the boss to waste his time and swear words on a young man he liked, sort of.

'I want you to speak to him now, Boss ...'

No response from the man as he continued to stare intently at some pictures on his laptop.

'... future CEOs MY ASS!' Snitchy ended her rants with a loud grunt.

That last part, the boss heard it clear and was not sure if it was spoken in exasperation, or as an enticement. A promising promise, nonetheless. A reminder too important to be ignored. That broke the good man's defences. Snitchy now had his total attention. Not wanting to take any chances, he took out his phone immediately.

'I hear you, Snitchy. Don't worry; will kick some MT butts today.'

Contacts: A, B, C, D ... M Me Meh Mehr

Incoming call: *Boss*

The one incoming call alert that always sent Meh's heart rate up every time though the man was always nice to him, sort of. Meh dropped his cigarette, got off the chair and stood in attention, as if the boss was standing right in front of him. The *paanwala* dropped a betel leaf with some slaked lime, got up along with him and stood in total attention, too, though Meh still does not know why.

'*Buggerrrr* ...' (The *deep* baritone that always sends heartbeats through the roof.)

'Yes, Boss, he-llo ... go-od morning.'

'Yeah, yeah ... hello. And yeah, morning morning.'

'What is happening in Kottayam, man?'

'We have a few cases in pipeline, Boss. But, errr …'

'But what? Pipeline what? You know I don't care a damn for stories, Mehraz. I need cheques and nothing else.'

'But Boss, Shibu … He seems to have a problem with our products and doesn't want to push our case much.'

'F@###r, if Shibu isn't *pushing*, what are you supposed to do? Sit and fart in the office the whole day? Use your effing brains, man. What did you do an MBA for? If things don't happen by this month end, I will effing hang you by your balls. All right? Okay, Snitchy will speak to you now. Talk to her and come up with something real. I need numbers coming in. Not pipelines, fancy s*** and *bleep, bleep* and a *bleep*. Bye.'

That was the first time anyone had used so many swear words on a young Mehraz without even an option of him returning them. He knew he should feel pathetic. He was about to, then …

Incoming call: *Snitchy Continental*

'*Ey! Hero*, what have you been doing all these days? Couldn't you have got your father's policy at least instead of warming your ass on egg crates, month after month?' Meh could hear a sarcastic grin over the phone. And a muffled laugh disguised as cough.

'But Continental tied up with MBL for their clients' policies, and not my father's, didn't they?'

'Smart-ass, tell that when you hear from the HR soon. All you MTs' necks are on the line. One more month of zero business, even Paddy or his daddy can't save you all. This is your last chance, dude. Listen, we have a lot of unique activities that are a real hit with MBL customers. Like painting competition for kids, lead-tracker book for MBL employees, referral schemes. Very unique and effective, you know. I designed them myself. We give them certificates and branded caps too.'

Caps and certificates. Sure, that will work. Why didn't you tell me about it earlier?

As if she heard Meh's silent sarcastic thoughts over the phone, she said:

'Or you can also come up with new ones and help the company, Mr Creative. CEO *aakendathu alle. Samayam illa, pettennu ayikkotte ...* [Don't you want to be the CEO soon? Hurry up.] CEOs, MY ASS!'

There was enough time after this call and before the next one for Meh to feel pathetic.

AN ANGELO DESCENDS

Shortly back in his seat, Meh saw that dignified elderly man in Shibu's office. He was always the most intelligent-looking man on the trading floor, even while doing something as unintelligent as short-selling. There was something about him that Meh felt was mysterious and attractive. Something about him reminded Meh of his father. It could be the age. The glasses. The receding hairline. That propensity for abstraction and philosophy. The kind who could only be a professor or a writer. Or, a retired professor or a failed writer. The kind who is totally at peace with himself, with the likelihood of having a son not totally so.

Meh had sketched this man's caricature in his sales diary. That was his favourite pastime in office, the only one. Drawing sketches of people—mostly caught in flight; frantically fleeing the insurance guy—and naming them. Then creating character sketches in his head as to what these people could be like in real life. And whenever he was introduced to any of them, they never matched his sketches. Do your sketches of strangers match their characters even after getting introduced to them? Or of acquaintances after getting to know them better? Or of people you count as close even after getting to know them fully?

Meh had named him 'Hollow Man.' He always walked past Meh as if he did not exist.

Then there was the 'Stripteaser.' A man in hitched-up dhoti who always gave the impression he was going to give Meh what he wanted—a new policy—but never does. He would shake his head dizzyingly; a quick swing between an uncertain *No* and an uninspiring *Yes*. Like a deceptive Tanjore doll, in a dhoti. A new excuse each time, but never a *No*. A firm *No* is always more helpful for any salesperson than an insincere *Yes*. Please note.

Then, the 'Hypocrite Communist' who continues to denounce all things bourgeoisie even while he bets on the shares of some large companies. And the 'Shy Bride,' the man who was always ill at ease, never made eye contact with Meh and would always draw mysterious patterns on the floor with his toes while speaking. And many others …

Hollow Man was only one of them. The only one of them who turned into Angelo.

'Mehraz, meet Angelo Sir.' There was something different in the way Shibu behaved with Angelo. An extra topping of cooked-up courtliness along with his usual subservience with all clients.

'Sir, this is Mehraz, our insurance *kid*.'

'I know. I have seen him around here. Come, sit.'

Regular pleasantries got exchanged half-heartedly. Unsure what Shibu's plan was that he had wanted Meh to play along, Meh was more focused on what Shibu had to say next.

'Sir, the kid is from a decent family. Nice chap, parents in respectable jobs and all. But unfortunately this one is a bit struggling. Has done MBA and all. But couldn't get a good job. Even this, he might lose soon. It is a bit pathetic. Please do something to help him, Sir.' A story said with such conviction, Shibu himself appeared overwhelmed by the plight of the young man in his own story, choking on his own deceptive words.

So this is it? Is this your big plan? Is this your major selling? All those brochures that talk about a Fortune 500 company, billions of funds under management, the Fitch ratings. All that flew right out of the window? All the portfolio management, broad-basing and stuff buried forever? It all boils down to me and my pathetic existence? A helpless Meh fumed within.

A future CEO in the works, armed with all possible business strategies, matrices and models, readying himself to make a global impact reduced to an object of charity in a blink. Whimsical dreams of a neophyte incapable of even dreaming the right dreams. Sales realities that bite. Meh felt like that strategically malnourished child he sees in the arms of the unrelenting wily lady at Kanjikkuzhy traffic signal every morning. Shibu, like the lady, had all ten fingers pointed at Meh and his malnourishment, attempting to draw an indifferent man's attention to his wretchedness; to conjure quick sympathy and money before the red light vanishes, the sympathy wanes and the man disappears. That desperate exhortation. That relentless extortion. A child forced to be, and to act, malnourished. Mehraz sat frozen. He was blank. Charmless and clueless.

Shibu looked at Meh like an actor nudging his co-actor to play his part; that too, after what he felt was the act of his life. Meh felt he should stand up and dispute all that the man had just said. To crash a laptop and bundle of brochures on the man's head and storm out. To stomp on a devious man lying spreadeagled on the floor adorned with a crown of broken laptop; leaflet clad. A thorn wreath. A crescent moon. A divine broker. The pent-up anger of all these days. An urchin and his egos.

A hartal day and its lectures crossed his mind. Meh ignored. An incoming call and a volley of abuse flashed in his head. *Effer* and effing, sitting and farting, balls and brains, bleep and bleep. Meh could not ignore it. Right there, at that precise moment, happened Meh's rite of passage into *salesmanhood*. Life was never the same again for Meh. Meh was never the same man in life again.

Meh gave Angelo the expression of a nice chap from a decent family with parents in respectable jobs, and all ... of one struggling after an MBA, and all ... of one who fails to get a good job, which he is likely to lose ... of one living a pathetic life and finally, of someone who needs help desperately. All of this, and one expression (for Meh to 'reflect it'). Meh nailed it.

'Give me your application form. Come to my office and collect the cheque today itself. Why delay the good?'

Shibu shook Angelo's hands. Angelo shook Meh's hands. Before leaving, Angelo handed over his business card asking Meh to meet him at four.

'Brilliant! I did it. Our branch's first policy. We are just starting off. We will be the first to get a policy in the region this month. I have a few more cases lined up.' Shibu's exultations while patting his own back. Like every successful salesman's.

Shibu walked out of his office this time. He called up his boss.

Meh remained. He did not know whom to call or where to walk to ...

11

AN OFFICE, TWO BOARDS

*A*nother desultory walk, but with an address to find this time. 4:03 p.m. Meh reached Angelo's office. There were two boards:

Bohemia Publishers Pvt Ltd, Erayilkadavu, Kottayam

Holy Faith Gold Loans Pvt Ltd, Erayilkadavu, Kottayam

One of the boards was old, dusty and dull. One office, two boards. Two businesses, no common denominators. Two names, many meanings. Like a man with multiple personality disorder. Like Meh. Like every man Meh knows. Multiple disorders, multiple personalities. Multiple personalities, no disorder. No disorder, no personality. Complex stuff, complex men. Forget it. But the mystery about the Hollow Man has just deepened.

'Come in, Mehraz.' Angelo lifted his head and took a break from rubbing gold on a black stone.

'I have kept the documents ready. See, I can invest about thirty-thousand every year. I would need some insurance cover and the remaining premium can go towards investments. Suggest a good plan for a 62-year-old based on this.'

Meh took out his blue book to find the right plan: Con Ass Lifetime Bliss. Ideal name for an insurance plan for a 62-year-old! Momentary lifetime indeed, its blisses too. An age where one usually regrets not having bought insurance and never really bothers to buy one. Meh flipped a few dozen pages; five dozen plus a two: *Six Teaaa Too*. This comes at the end of the premium table. Buried hidden in the forgotten folds of every blue book there is. Where one of those obscure elements no one has any use of could be hiding in a periodic table.

Premium Rs 29,279 every year for ten years. Coverage for twenty-five years! An optimistic actuary.

> Pay: Continental Assurance India Pvt Ltd. Rs 29,279. Sd/-Angelo.

The first cheque. Sales is not that difficult, after all. Meh felt elated and hopeful. He knew he should act elated and hopeful. He could not. But he was alive again, relieved too.

The first is always special. It is always the most difficult, too. It can take a long time coming. And it is always misery until it comes. Be it sales deals, love, poems or just about anything in life. (The first deal took more than four sales-months for the dazed MT. The love, twenty-two years and the poetry, another seventeen more years—or what he assumed was love and poetry.) Then it will all keep coming so easily: deals, love, poems, paintings, software codes, jobs, money, lies, friends, girlfriends, boyfriends, swimming, riding bicycles, flying airplanes ... So easy that you wonder what the difficulty was in the first place. You get so good at it over time, it becomes so natural for you to get it. Then it gets difficult for you not to get it. Sometimes impossible to get out of, or to rid of. The perfection that comes with practice. The contempt that comes with familiarity. Everything is as easy or as hard. Only perspectives change based on the vantage point one looks at things from. One just needs to bide one's time to get to that point.

Meh wanted to thank Angelo and wished to know the real reason why this man opted to buy a policy. He was taught that only a man who is sure to die will ever voluntarily buy life insurance. Are there people who are not sure to die? Or sure not to? Is this man contemplating suicide? Does he have a terminal illness that he wants to hide? Meh wondered. He also wanted to know the story behind the two boards in his office.

Meh couldn't say or ask anything further. Angelo bade him a quick goodbye and went back to rubbing gold on a black stone more vigorously. Like a detective trying to uncover the hidden lies in an ornamented piece of yellow metal. He was a man of few words, Meh thought. After all, what does a Shylock have to talk about? Meh was also happy to leave.

'There will be a medical examination shortly.' Meh told Angelo as he was leaving. Meh was sure the medical tests will bring out the truth even if the man does not want to divulge now. Like gold on touchstone.

An amount of Rs 29,279 is not very big. It is bigger than zero, but not as big as a million rupees. It is about a third of Meh's monthly target. More importantly, it is a start. It goes a long way to help keep his job and dignity. Sometimes, it is not about the quantum. It is about what it is and when it happens. The spell has been broken. Meh has tasted blood. He is off zero. He is not a nothing anymore. It is a redemption, no doubt; no matter how brief.

'You have insured a certain risk, Mehraz; totally taken out of the equation all the probability calculations that we pay the actuaries a bomb for. Anyway, good start. But, this is *No Big Deal!* You know that, right? Get some bigger deals. See if he has a son or grandson of a more insurable age and sell more. He sure will have. *Chalo*, long way to go.' Territory manager got off the call. Meh was not sure if the call was appreciatory or accusatory. He missed the *theris*.

An Office, Two Boards

Meh called his mother. He wanted to thank her for her constant prayers that he believed had the power to manifest cheques. It was to be a routine from then on.

'*Amma,* how are you doing?'

The greeting and the script seem to have become a part of Mehraz's life by now.

'Nothing. I was *chumma* reading the encyclopaedia. You should also take one with you the next time you come.'

'Why are you *reading* an encyclopaedia? And why do you have another one?'

'Oh! There was this kid who came yesterday. Lanky, dark fellow with glasses and all. A bag and tie also, just like you. Why do all *you people* even wear it, Meh? Anyway, I thought of you and felt bad … how my son also must be going around like this, door to door, in that strange town. I just felt like helping him and prayed that at least the mothers there took some sympathy on my son. I can't say *No* to any salesperson these days. You know, I bought half a dozen *agarbatis* and two vegetable choppers too.' All the queries and updates in one breath, like all mothers.

'Good. Thank you, *Amma*. Will call you later tonight.'

Congratulatory mails, commission calculations, cake cutting and admiring glances from a non-squint eye at MBL office.

No Bigg Deal!

An incomplete gratitude, a question about two boards and a buyer's intent haunted Meh.

About neckties too ...

A MAN, MANY WORDS, DIRTY SECRETS

8:53 a.m. [Divine Diagnostics, Baker Junction]

The medical examination was scheduled for 9:00 a.m. Angelo had to be on a 12-hour fast for the test. Meh arrived early and waited for Angelo. 9:37 a.m. No signs of Angelo. Meh was certain that the man was trying to dodge the medical test. Like every man who has something to hide, unable to face up to the truths. Like every man scared to face one's own thoughts and dodges them always. (A short YouTube video, a needless scroll up and down Insta Reels, that routine checking of WhatsApp messages not received. The dodgers that we are.)

There is nothing much one can do to kill time at a diagnostic centre. Meh looked around. People impatiently waiting to be pricked. A snug cobweb—an intricately woven snare—with enough flies trapped for a hearty meal. A lizard with no web, above a board, waiting for flies. The board caught Meh's eye: 'Does your child have behavioural issues? Does he always prefer to be alone? Does he always keep away from crowds? Special psychiatry clinic on the first Friday of every month. Kottayam's most famous psychiatrist, Dr D'Souza, available at Divine Diagnostics.'

At what point does normal behaviour turn into a disorder? Who decides the point? Who decides the disorder? Who decides the normal? What makes D'Souza believe these are all behavioural issues that need *cure*? What makes the world believe that everyone who avoids crowds or lives behind closed doors is a psychopath, a pothead, a serial killer or a serial masturbator? Or someone planning to be one, or all. A Standard Pill: An easy answer—to all purposeful existential questions of a man. A simple cure—to all vexing existential issues of mankind. To lull to sleep every mind that yearns for an awakening. To bring in conformity for all non-conforming minds.

Meh felt he should burn down that misplaced board on the way down for his next smoke. Like a psychopath! Thoughts that kill time. Reverse, too. Beware!

Angelo arrived at 10:16 a.m. despite appearing to have rushed, like everyone else. Meh was more worried about a diabetic like Angelo skipping his breakfast. The man's insurance is yet to be active too. Can a claim precede the medical test? Meh wasn't sure. But he knew human life is precious. More precious than his targets and too valuable to put a price to, even if a claim was to be paid.

A Man, Many Words, Dirty Secrets

Meh told him, 'Sir, forget the medical test. It is okay, or if you don't mind, I will get it rescheduled for a later date. Why don't you go have your breakfast?'

This would mean Meh potentially losing his only business and also not getting to know about this man's dirty secret that he was keen to know. The red flag that he was warned about by his underwriter who sees red flags in just about everything. An underwriter who seemed to know everything about every man's dirty secrets. About longevity, too.

'That is okay. I can handle this. I took this policy only to help you. Let it not go to waste. Let's get this done with and have breakfast together. Why delay the good, Mehraz?'

A Shylock with a heart! The character sketches, the red flags, the moral hazards, the certain deaths and dirty secrets. How wrong are we almost always about another? How unwilling are we to accept that someone can be genuinely noble without an agenda? Expectations that never match realities. Character sketches that never match characters. An underwriter's assumptions that never match the outcomes. How many wrong assumptions before we realise how good can someone be? The underwriters, the judges, the knowers that we are.

Meh had his answer even before the medical test. Now he only had one more question to ask. And a thank-you to say.

Hotel Aaryaas. Right below the diagnostic centre. Masala dosas and vadas.

'So, how is life, Mehraz?'

'Business has been bad, Sir. Pressures are ...'

'I asked about life, Mehraz. Two different things, aren't they?'

A Shylock who knows the difference! Not bad.

'Oh, I was just answering the easy one. Life ... too young to figure out, I suppose.'

'Who told you *the old* figure it out? Age has nothing to do with it. How old was Jesus and how old was Joseph? Only one of them figured out. Clue: he died much younger.'

A Shylock who talks! Interesting.

'I know from Mini about your struggles. Forget Shibu, he will never change. You are too young. Don't give up so easily. You are just getting started and at your age, there are endless possibilities. Every young man your age is like a fruit with many seeds. Each of them, a possibility that will sprout and bloom when the time is right. One just has to be willing to let go of the certainties, and embrace the possibilities.'

Meh felt there was someone in that town who understands him, finally. And perhaps, all that he does not understand, too.

'What do you want to be in life, Mehraz?'

'I have no idea, Sir. But I definitely don't want to be in sales. I am pathetic at it.'

'Says who? Isn't it a bit too early for conclusions? Always remember, if you are not good at what you are doing now, it does not mean you are not good at everything you are not doing, too. You will do well in what you ought to be doing. The bigger problem is when you start doing well in what you should not be doing. That would bring a misery deeper than the misery of not doing well in what you should not be doing. So … what are you good at?'

Meh understood nothing of what the man just spoke. Except the last question. And that … that was one question he never had an answer to. One he always wished he had had.

'Oh, I am not bad at a lot of things. But you know, never good enough. I love to play cricket. I play the guitar. I love to sing. I can paint. I love to write. Never good enough. But one thing I just can't do is selling. I don't like it either, and that is what I have to do. Maybe I will switch to something else soon, HR or something. I don't know; it is never easy to change tracks. If nothing works, and if I feel I have reached the end of the road, I know what needs to be done. Like every desperate man like me … I will also … move to some foreign country …'

'That almost sounded suicidal, Mehraz.' Angelo smiled a rare, hesitant smile. 'Wherever you are stuck, be happy. If you do well, be happy that you are doing well. If you do bad, be happy that you are doing bad because you will get out sooner. You will one day feel thankful for this sense of void within, the constant feeling of *something missing*. Because that is what will lead you to where you should be. Don't mind if you are in a dark phase now, like a free fall into a fathomless abyss. The darker it is today, the brighter your tomorrows will be. The deeper you fall, the higher you soar. You will have wings of fire, Mehraz. Every human does …'

Angelo sounded just like every preacher who preaches to the wrong audience. Not that the preacher is wrong. It might be the wrong timing. Oh no, I admit; it could be the audience itself.

Meh was quick to cut him off. He had already missed a few calls from an underwriter, and a Shibu.

'Sir, right now my bottom is on fire. All this philosophy is good at your age. Let me finish breakfast and rush to the office. I am already late. I will speak to you once your policy is active.' Meh got up, ready to rush.

'Sure, Mehraz ...'

A word of gratitude remained unsaid. A question, unasked ...

SALES WINS CONTINUE, BUT WHY?

With time, things were getting easier for Meh. A few more sales wins. The good thing about sales is that you don't have to do anything more if your targets are achieved. The bad thing about sales is that there is nothing much you can do if your targets are not achieved—too many uncontrollable variables and you are too much at the mercy of others. The worst thing about sales is that you have nothing more to do if your targets are achieved. Ask any successful sales guy, he will explain. We move on.

With Meh growing in confidence and Shibu in greed, they started hunting for bigger deals. An NGO was looking for investment options for its employees, about 20 of them. Too small to elicit any interest from institutional business guys. Too big for individual business guys like Meh to not show any interest. They were looking for investments with duration of less than five years, while all of Continental's products were designed for fifteen years and more. But

Sales Wins Continue, but Why?

Shibu had his own crafty ways of packaging and selling these long-term plans for shorter durations. What some call as mis-selling, Shibu prefers to call it smart-selling. The man in charge was Mr Sherief. Pious, forthright and tough, he was giving the insurers a hard time. Shibu, for some odd reason, was confident that Meh could crack this guy. Under his tutelage, of course.

A few meetings done. Politics, religion, weather, sports, interstellar travel; very little of sales talks and a lot of tea, as it happens in most client meetings. A decision was to be taken shortly. Shibu always dropped hints about a 'struggling-nice-chap-from-decent-family.' One with an MBA, a pathetic existence, and all.

One day Sherief asked Shibu about Meh's targets.

'Twelve lakh for the year, Sir. A lakh a month.'

'Is that all? He has a million-dollar smile. He can easily do a few lakhs with that smile alone.'

That sounded so wrong. Meh did not smile this time, fearing it would be construed as solicitation. He ignored the man's words. In sales, as in life, *ignoring* is bliss. The joke itself was off. The logic, too. Meh had heard from his female colleagues stories of uncomfortable advances and overtures made by clients. He had always felt sympathetic about it. This just felt pathetic. Why me? Meh wondered.

'Ha! Ha! Ha!' Shibu laughed. Loud. Perhaps to show that he also had a smile and a laugh. At least half a million rupees?

'Do you have any work with the *kid* after this? I would need him for about an hour, if you don't mind ...'

'Most certainly! Take him, all yours.' Shibu was more than happy giving Meh away even before Sherief could complete.

'... we have a prayer group that assembles here for the *namaz* on some days. I was hoping that Meh could join us today.' Meh felt relieved. He was about to heave a sigh of relief. He paused. *It is okay, at least it is not as bad as what I imagined.* He then heaved half a sigh of relief and stuck around hesitantly.

'Come, son. Let's go.' Sherief got up and started preparing to go for the *namaz*.

Meh felt resentful knowing that Shibu would have most certainly said 'most certainly' even if Sherief's request was for whatever Meh had dreaded. Shibu's plan was simple, and heinous. He was always looking for ways to get the devout Mr Sherief to take a liking to the not-at-all-religious Meh. At least half a liking, given that Meh was at least half a Muslim on his father's side. Shibu had reasoned in his head.

Shibu was keen to know if there was anything else about Meh that would make him appear more religious than he actually is. *Halal pork*? At least reciting the sacred invocation—In the name of the creator who *forbideth*, we *drinketh* ...—before the first sip at Ambassador every evening? He stopped short of asking some uncomfortable questions about covenants and promises, sacrifices and forsaken skins; as if after some forethought.

'Go ahead. People do far worse to get sales.' Shibu slyly prodded a hesitant Meh.

Play along, act along has anyway been the message for Meh since that Monday. He decided to play along. To act along. To do far worse ...

At the *namaz*, Meh ensured he was alone in the last row so that no one could see him mimic the man in front. But Meh wasn't aware that the *Imam*, the elderly man leading the prayer, would finish first. He noticed Meh's acrobatics as he was leaving the congregation. After it was all done and the others had left, the *Imam* asked Meh, 'You really don't have much of an idea, do you?'

Not the novice salesman at *Appachan*'s house anymore, Meh was quick to respond: 'Well, I have always wanted to ... but my father being an almost atheist, I never could. And the missionary school I went to, all this wasn't allowed either.' The topic suddenly changed as the *Imam* spoke to Sherief about 'them' monopolising education and how 'our' kids end up 'straying' as a result. The easy wedges, the silly schisms. Us and them. Theirs and ours. Divide and rule. Easy *and* peasy. Even for a 23-year-old. Meh realised he was not that innocent anymore. Here, he almost triggered a second crusade, a millennium later. Or was Meh's answer the reflection of a truth he never knew?

The deal kept swinging. Meh wanted it badly and was not willing to give up now. He now had two of the key decision-makers on *his side*; of the schism—an invisible yet evident one. He downloaded a government report on the socio-economic status of Indian minority groups, and went through it in detail; a robber planning his next heist. For him it only meant client engagement and talking points. Meh shunned Shibu for meetings and started engaging with the client directly, speaking passionately on the government report about the plight of *our* brothers and also on the RBI economic report about the plight of *the* economy, as the situation demanded. Both with equal ease. He was getting better.

Nineteen policies with an annualised premium of Rs 25,000 each: Rs 4,75,000.

Approx. '0.5' million rupees

Approx. '5' in terms of Meh's monthly targets

Approx. '1' estimated in terms of a Shibu's smile

Sales Wins Continue, but Why?

Longer congratulatory mails, complex commission calculations, bigger cakes and stronger admiring glances at MBL office. Shibu topped his region by a huge margin. He won a laptop as a prize from Continental; his own *entheppenadi*. Everyone else got freshly dusted caps and certificates from an almost disused drawer. Pre-signed certificates where *appreciators* do not know names of the *appreciated*. A happy Snitchy. Certified Happy.

Everyone and everything around seemed to be celebrating his success at being a failure, Meh felt. Things were beginning to get comfortable for him in office. Mini *Chechi's* eyes did not have that sympathy for him anymore. It was not needed. She thanked her god for having answered her prayers. An extra candle lighted. The Pretty One continued to look pretty. There was a special gleam on her one eye that has been sparkling brighter of late. She had saved that only for Meh, stealing glances more often. She would look at everyone else with the squinted eye at the same time in a disorienting sort of way, and hence no one noticed the gleam on her other eye for Meh. Except one man ...

Das had always disliked Meh, now all the more. He believed there once was a special gleam, saved only for him. Now she looks at him also with the squinted eye, the same way she looks at everyone else. He does everything possible; to win back that gleam, to charm her again. There is no man more pitiful to watch than the one who wrongly believes he has a woman under his charm. A deluded snake charmer. He swings, he sways; he gyrates, he blows his own out-of-tune trumpet. The snake does her own thing that he perceives as being entranced. J. U. Das continued to be the snake charmer on a trading floor …

Meh was not too happy about the success. The deeper, inexplicable miseries of *success* unlike the easier, obvious miseries of *failure*. Something was amiss. Meh had no idea what it was and the distances he will have to travel before he gets to know what it is. But he was certain that this was not where he belonged; that this was only a brief sojourn before he figured out where he should get to. This sort of success is dangerous. Like a wayfarer getting too comfortable at the night inn. Comforts that make him lose sight of his destination. It is better to be a failure in what you do not like than to be a winner, Meh remembered Angelo's words. It began making sense.

Many a time, people choose to continue to walk on the wrong path. Sometimes they run fast hoping they can get out sooner; they only burn out faster. For they are scared to pause, scared to walk back. Scared of lost time and distances already covered. Scared to choose a new path, they continue to trudge, even when knowing it is the wrong path. One wrong turn after the other, as if rushing to reach some final point of no return. Like a lost wayfarer following another's confused footprints on deceptive desert sands. Leaving fresh ones for the ones behind. A lost trail …

Meh showered. Ambassador beckoned. Alcohol … that which liberates every slave temporarily and enslaves every free man, forever. A distressed salesman to vodka-sodden optimist. *One-nightly stands* with optimism.

Meh was the only one his age at Ambassador, most of the time. He was the only one who was alone too, always. Everyone else had family, or friends. Or they made friends there. Everyone else is with people, you alone are alone. (Good or bad? Think.) Which is a bigger tragedy: not being able to put food on the plate for loved ones or not having loved ones to share your food with? (Sure? You might want to think again.) Pains that can never be meaningfully shared. Joys that need to be shared to be meaningful. Deprivation. Aloneness. Solitude. Aloneness that makes every young man susceptible to liquor, libido and food poisoning, before some learn to transmute it into solitude. Then the solitude makes a few susceptible to love, poetry and philosophy and they transfigure from men to humans or from hopeless salesmen to hopeful writers …

In the dark room of a *tharavadu* house, the darkness darkened and the silence swelled. Meh checked online for some calming music. His friend had told that it helped her sleep faster. 'Fall asleep in three minutes.' Clickbait for videos that had duration of over eight hours. Something did not add up. Distorting long-term benefit as short term seems to be a marketing ploy everywhere, not just in his industry. Meh looked in the mirror that night under the light of a flickering bulb. The mirror is like a good friend. An honest friend who tells you how ugly you are.

What am I?

An impostor? A hypocrite? A hustler? Or just a good salesman in the making?

Meh realised he was beginning to be good at being bad. And that was scary.

And that had to end.

… Is there a man more bound than the one who doesn't know he is bound?

A GOOD SAMART ARRIVES

There were only two people who wore black suits in that town; both men, a source of joy and of hope. Two men capable of taking Meh out of that burrow of despair. One, momentarily; the other, potentially. First one was the bartender at Ambassador. He was too skilled for a bar like that, for a town like this. He used to be in Dubai and was unwilling to believe that he is back in Kerala. Having so many Keralites around only made things worse. He would spend an awfully long time showing off his bartending skills that the despondent men would always frown, *'Oh! ennaa parayaanaanne, maduppiraanenne';* sitting hunched around rubber-wood tables, collectively dredging up deep-rooted apathy, with broken toothpicks.

The second one was Samart, a cousin of Meh's friend, from Bangalore. He is an institutional sales guy who works for the largest private insurance company. He carries an office-provided laptop and is known to deliver impressive boardroom presentations. Meh was dejected that his own amateurish presentations those days never had any *mature content*, while everything else he used his personal laptop for, did. Like every other man in that town who uses a personal laptop. That had to end, too.

If it is sales, it has to be institutional sales, Meh believed. If it is insurance, it has to be with the market leader, Meh liked to believe. If it is a tie, it has to be with a suit, Meh still believes. Tie without a suit makes one feel half naked, full shy, total salesman-like. After all, is there a management graduate who does not wish to give boardroom presentations in a suit? What else do they wish to do? What else can they wish to do?

Samart was a good man with a big heart and a congested chest. An exceptional salesman, he was aggressive, sophisticated and asthmatic. The kind who can walk out of an Ashram *bhajan* onto a dance floor with equal poise. Half Goan, half Bengali. Can there be any two better halves that can join to make a better, fuller Indian?—the Brain, the Cheer; Bhakti and Beer; Rabi and Remo. He was here for a meeting with an old newspaper company for a deal worth a few hundred crores. Meh did not even mention his half a million deal. He felt too dwarfed and insignificant. Meh's friend had asked him if he was willing to work with Samart. That natural progression to institutional business. That default dream for most sales guys in individual business. It was *one small step for any salesman, but a giant leap for the Meh kind.*

There was one man who believed Meh could not do it. That was Meh himself. It was always so. Everyone else seemed better than him, especially during those days. These kind of jobs are meant only for smart men like Samart, Meh believed. A pesky ghost in his head also kept whispering so. He always saw faceless school friends from a small town blow raspberries every time he acted *smart*, felt unseen fingers tug at the back of his shirt each time he stood up to speak his mind or while delivering presentations. Are these ghosts faithfully wedded only to him, or others also carry them on their backs? Meh always wondered. Small-town peeps; big problems, peeps. Problems that the Samarts would never understand.

But Samart's visits were a relief. He gave Meh some company and a lot of hope. Also, Meh was always fascinated about this man who flies in and out of cities and his stories about large corporates and large deals. Like a prisoner enchanted by a wanderer's stories. About unfettered freedom and infinite horizons. An undying desire for freedom that encourages every man to dream. Restless human imagination that refuses to be bound by high walls and barbed wires. Or card access turnstiles.

On a Friday evening, Meh took Samart to Ambassador and Hobnob. There was nowhere else to take him to. They had a lot of beer that night. There was nothing else to do in that town either. The bond got stronger. Is there anything that makes human bonds warmer than cold beer? Or triggers wheezing? ... Beer, humidity, outlandish suit, copious sweat and the sultry Kerala weather being unkind to a man used to Bangalore's balmy weather; Samart fell ill. It triggered his wheezing. He stayed an extra day in Kottayam. In between all the coughing and wheezing, while using his inhaler profusely and expelling generous amount of phlegm, Samart asked Meh, who had the earnestness of a good nurse, if he wished to join Samart's team. Meh was not sure. He never was.

'We will do it when you can breathe first.' Meh dodged it. He knew he wanted it badly. He just did not know if he was good enough. Samart decided to get to the neighbouring city on Sunday morning. He felt choked there. Like Meh. Like everyone else. He was coughing so hard even when he got in the car. (Input: Corticosteroids; Output: Mucous matter. A well-oiled human machine.) He struggled to get out even to spit. A waiting Meh cupped his hands and *pleaded* with the earnestness of a nurse and the subservience of a Shibu: 'Boss-to-be, give it here. I will trash it.'

Samart laughed out loud. (He always had an infectious laugh.) He coughed louder. (Okay, that remains infected even today.)

'You are a jolly good fella. You will fit right in. I will wait for your call.' He spluttered.

Meh wondered what the joke was.

A BEAUTIFUL PROMISE (ALMOST). THE END (ALMOST)

*T*his cannot continue. This has to end. It does feel bad to let it continue like this. An inexperienced salesman, like an unaccomplished writer. Apologetic, reticent. Aloof, hesitant. About unsolicited calls and words. About unwanted requests and favours. Okay, this is a good point to end it with.

It was to be a big meeting that evening. Meh knew from the red tie and serious look on Shibu's face. And for important meetings these days, Shibu carries his own *entheppenadi* that he got from Continental. 'Carry some brochures. Big customer, Meh. You should not ask for anything less than a lakh. Or should it be two?'

Not every NRI waits for Christmas. Tina did not. She came with the first showers of monsoon that year. A healthy monsoon after a failed monsoon the previous year

A Beautiful Promise (Almost). The End (Almost)

and a scorching Indian summer that never fails. She was the daughter of another big client of Shibu's. They were a family of doctors in New York. Dr Tina. That completes it. No, it does not.

Shibu and Mehraz were greeted in by a man who looked just like every man who is a doctor and has a beautiful daughter to protect. Watchful and protective, almost territorial. He was Dr Richard, Tina's *Appa*. He kept talking about his plans for his daughter and wanted Shibu to help her develop a savings habit. Insurance made a lot of sense, he said. That, for any prospect to say, is a rarity. That sure helps.

Tina was all that an attractive girl her age could be. She was full of life and seemed to not have a care about anything in this world. A long curl of hair carelessly caressing her face; a black mole above dewy lips that looked like wine drop trapped in crystal. Wide starry eyes, she had colourful dreams sparkle in them. She smiled the most striking of smiles. A smile that always elicits a smile from the other—at the sight or the thought of it. A smile that remains even after the person has left—the fragrance that lingers even after a flower has been plucked. She was black. She was beautiful, too. *Nah!* All this just won't do. Let me try that again:

Tina! She was black … She was beautiful … She was beautiful in a way black alone can be beautiful … That's it.

She emerged fresh from her shower, floating down a flight of stairs into the living room. A dark, serene cloud descending from an evening monsoon sky. Droplets of sweat and water still dazzled on her glistening dark skin, dripping from her hair onto her shoulders and then on a trail down the contours of her body. Thoughts, taking nebulous shapes, ready to go on a free fall along with those droplets—like how they do inside a writer's head. (Trickles: of letters, stray thoughts and plots. Buried, vague and garbled. Then, that deep dive into the hidden recesses of self … that deluge of clear words, ideas and stories. Desirable ones. That relief! All, only if he gets it right.) A young man was ready to follow the droplets on their journey to the nether regions of hidden beauty. He was unsure which one to follow, what thoughts to pursue. Treasures hidden that make a man want to go on a treasure hunt in his head, guided only by a vague mental map. Feeling envious of the one who would eventually make it, if he does not. Shameful thoughts. That sin! All the blames, only if he does not make it.

The only problem with dreams is that they are dreams. Until they become realities; until they become real, like dreams. Dreams that do come true …

A beautiful voice brought him back to his present realities.

'Oh! So good to see some familiar names and younger faces. Other than GIC and that nagging old agent. I have

A Beautiful Promise (Almost). The End (Almost)

like literally all my insurances with you guys back in the U.S. In fact, your office is right across the street from where I work.'

'Madison Avenue?'

'Yep. Hi! Tina Richard.'

'Mehraz ...'

'Shee Buu!'

'Mr Shibu, I know. You are *Appa's* most trusted man in the whole of Kottayam.'

A lousy knot on a red tie was tightened. A face, a tummy swelled and blushed with pride.

'See, I don't get all this. I will totally go by what *Appa* says. Just tell me how much to invest and where to sign. And if you can show me something on a spreadsheet with some basic numbers, that would be awesome. Keep it simple and sweet, please.'

Shibu pushed the *entheppenadi* towards Meh. Meh pushed the brochures towards Shibu.

'Mickeymouse@1'

'... am sorry?'

'The password, Mehraz. M is capital letters, okay? Data security, you know.'

Meh realised at that moment that one should never get to know a wannabe alpha male's hidden fears, or his password.

Shibu wrote '2' on a piece of paper and circled it. He then crossed it out, wrote '1.5' and tapped a ringed index finger on it. Meh ignored.

Meh input a ten. Ten lakh. A million rupees. As if in redemption of a broken promise of a million rupees. A simulation, a presentation that a prospect actually saw. A million rupees that could well become a reality. Meh made a passionate appeal, as if down on one knee. And she said Yes! Yes! and a Yes!

Appa nodded his approval. 'Come and collect the documents and cheque the day after.'

'Anything that helps me retire by forty.' Tina beamed. Another twenty-something-year-old planning retirement. Meh liked that, too.

Eloquent, defenceless eyes that unwittingly revealed more than they could hide. A beautiful oyster happily yielding its pearls. Lips that conveyed with a smile things beautiful that words never can. A warm handshake that lingered comfortably too long. A few Mississippis and some longer Connecticuts too. Meh counted, borrowing from how they count their seconds around Madison Avenue.

A Beautiful Promise (Almost). The End (Almost)

Two happy men, happy for different reasons, went their separate ways that evening through unlit roads devoid of streetlights.

... Bakery & Cool Bar, Rubber Traders, Travel Agents, Darkness ...

... Darkness, Travel Agents, Rubber Traders, Bakery & Cool Bar ...

A BEAUTIFUL PROMISE THAT NEVER WAS

The day after. MBL office. A Shibu—a Shibu, like a thousand other Shibus—was missing. No one knew where this one went. No one wanted to know either. A man, if he is a magician, the crowd wishes he forgets the trick to do the reappearing act after a disappearing act. That kind of man. That kind of boss. For everyone; not for Meh, not today.

A fidgety Meh kept looking through the corner of his eye for a belly and its appendage. A trading floor that was chaotic as usual. 11:34 a.m. A red tie and a human body to support it walked in and placed itself on a chair. Then a laptop on a table. A Shibu settled down. Meh could wait no longer or would want to waste any more time.

'Shouldn't we go back for finishing the documentation?' Meh asked excitedly, standing by Shibu's office door. He still hates stepping inside that office.

'Miniye, aa aathmarthatha kando? Njaan paranjillayirunno?' [Mini, you see that dedication? Didn't I tell you?]

Mini *Chechi* gave Shibu a half-smile and Meh a full-stare. Like how she would look at someone who had broken all ten of the commandments.

'*Onnum venda*. No need. I just picked it up today morning. Why don't you go follow up on that 67-year-old *Ammachi's* proposal? You are anyway an expert on geriatric insurance.' Shibu had a smirk and a set of documents. That same smirk from a Friday evening. Same evil one, minus the pastry flake.

Meh ignored this jibe, too. Over time, sales makes you immune to such insults—an induced meekness, an inability to react. It is as if you develop antibodies against insults from the constant exposure. Like how you do against a pestilent virus. Like chickenpox. Meh walked back to his seat. He rummaged through the documents that had her passport copy, some other IDs and a photograph. She looked beautiful in all of them. Can anyone look so pretty on a government ID? Can anyone smile so cheerful in a studio, even when knowing it is for some sad official document? Meh hurried to look for something very important in the proposal form, something more important than a million-rupee cheque.

A croaky voice cut short Meh's futile pursuits.

'Just so you know, that mobile number is of her uncle in Devalokam and that email ID, that is mine. Richard Sir has asked me to operate the account on their behalf. They are all leaving for Cochin tomorrow and then onward to the U.S. in a week. On an airplane …'

As always, he then turned to Mini *Chechi*. '*Ketto Miniye*, someone feels that someone in our office is smart. Too smart to be in a place like Kottayam, it seems. *Enthaa le?* She didn't have as many questions about the policy as she had about our young MT. Big impressions and all someone creates on people, eh?' *Hi! Hi! Hi!* A weird sound. Meh realised it was Shibu's giggle. Of contempt mixed with contentment.

All that remained of Tina was a photograph, and a promise. All that remains of Tina is the memory of a photograph, and of a promise. And some questions, too, just like she had …

A young salesman vowed never to start a client meeting without exchanging business cards. At least without leaving behind his own. He was learning.

Meh stepped out.

While placing the *sutta* on the *dabba*, the *paanwala* told Meh that he is leaving town shortly. To a faraway town. In a truck.

He gave Mehraz the *flame*. Meh took out his phone.

'Hello, Samart …'

AN INTERLUDE BEFORE THE ACTUAL END

*M*ehraz, the dazed management trainee, is now a manager handling institutional sales, following Samart's footsteps. Unaware that he is following another's confused footsteps, unaware of that man's miseries. Impersonating a successful man: the new role for the clueless actor. And the domino fell in Mumbai, not Bangalore; and a different boss, not Samart. All for unknown reasons, again. From the warmth and promises of living rooms to the cold and boredom of boardrooms. From the darkness of a sleepy town to the neon hues of a bustling metropolis that never sleeps. Pubs and cafes took the place of Ambassador and Hobnob. Big city, bigger clients. Big cheques, bigger void.

Meh continued to remain meh as ever, doing Meh things. And like most people who don't have much talent or put any heart into what they do, Meh was successful. Okay, Meh received enough cheques and that equates with success in that world, too. The *Best Seller*. Meh was beginning to forget everything about Kottayam. Angelo was the only one who took the effort to keep in touch. Meh forgot everyone else. Everyone else forgot Meh.

One evening Meh receieved a group mail announcing that year's annual sales conference. A yearly stagey event where it is a repeat of that glitzy hotel and propagandas all over again. And a lot of alcohol. The MT has become a salesman now and alcohol was officially permitted, not just *chaai biskoot*. Alcohol that helps make a sale, and a man. Conferences where a lot of drinking, celebrating meaningless successes and vilifying harmless failures happen. Reviews and previews, postmortems and prophecies, applauding and accusing. Then in the night, sharing bedrooms with strange men from another part of the country in an effort to build team synergies overnight. An almost-jobless HR loves playing cupid and insists on such matchmaking. Meh hated that the most, along with everything else.

The invite was equally sad: 'Two days of fun and frolic in the most exotic of all locations in God's own country. No prizes for guessing. *Yayyyyy!* Kumarakom, the palm-fringed paradise in the land of Coconuts and Three Ls. Latex, L——'

Thenga! Coconuts!!!! Meh did not even read it fully. He shut his laptop.

Sometimes, we leave behind what the world counts as exotic and the world can never see why.

Sometimes, we embrace as exotic what the world leaves behind and the world will never see why.

Back to Kottayam, after many years. Not out of his choice, even this time. At the conference, Meh skipped most sessions, developing a skill to camouflage, to be inconspicuous; to be alone in a crowd. The second night was the *gala night*. Celebrations and awkwardness were at their peak.

Deprived men granted free access to alcohol and women. Desperate men who can't hold their liquor and thoughts making unsuccessful advances at uninterested women. Alcohol made them believe they were knock-off Don Juans, for a night. Insecure employees struggling to hold conversations with uninterested senior management, hoping for names and impressions to be registered. Alcohol made that CXO appear as if he was genuinely interested. Many random people were seen posing for pictures—with 'the *most* prestigious' award trophies they give out to *most* people—intended for indiscriminate social circulation. They all use the same expressions and the same captions, to express *vain* contentment. Then, Meh saw at a distance, Mr Sharma, that respected gentleman during office hours, pretending as if he was dry humping a pole. Alcohol made Mr Sharma believe he

An Interlude before the Actual End

was being funny. The difference between Mr Sharma and Mr *Besharma* is but a peg of whisky.

Meh sneaked out. He wished he had not seen any of it. Sleep was better, eyes firmly shut. Meh was fast asleep in his room. His phone kept ringing continuously, like an upset girlfriend trying to wake him up with the constant buzzing. There were multiple missed calls; from his new boss and Samart. He sounded happy and worried at once:

'Where are you, Meh? *Arre*, you won the Star of the Year award. Congrats. You are screwed but. Come fast.'

Star what? Come where? Screwed why?

A sleepy Meh manifested on a podium. An almost-forgotten, promising young man from Bangalore whose name remains *unrecallable* had received the Star of the Year award the previous year. At age 28. At 29, he was dead. Celebrated the previous year, forgotten the next. Died on his wedding anniversary, a month before his son's first birthday. (I tried, I still can't recollect his name.) The spotlight was on Mehraz now. He rubbed his sleepy eyes—that dazed Meh expression. With all the lights beaming on him, he felt like a nun under the spotlight in a strip club. Totally out of place. Totally unsure of his next move. All he wanted was some darkness to cover himself. He missed a dark *tharavadu* house with tiled roof and a flickering bulb, not too far from there. Everyone, right from the CEO, noticed how uncomfortable this one was about being under the spotlight. Award handed over mechanically, award received mechanically, smug photo expression extracted successfully. In the background, someone rushed through insincere scripted praise for yet another promising salesman before abandoning it halfway and rushing to the bar counter.

Backstage, a drowsy actor who missed his act reproached by his new boss, yet again. A deviant who upsets team synergies by choosing to drink alone, and sleep alone. A flaccid salesman whom no certificates, awards, appreciatory mails, cakes or any known stimulants could excite. The boss was already tired of trying to get this one to appear less meh. Too sophisticated to be using swear words, he was refined and surgical. He stripped Meh slowly. Then skinned him, one layer at a time. Like a benevolent butcher. Meh felt he missed the *theris*.

Meh was in no hurry to get back to Mumbai. He decided to stay an extra day in Kottayam and catch up with Angelo. He still had a thank-you to offer and a question to ask; maybe drop by MBL and Continental offices, too. With time, even Kottayam was beginning to be a warm memory. Like how the once-hated schools and the colourful memories of a black-and-white Doordarshan did, over time.

Mile sur meraa tumhaara … Ek titli, anek titliyaan …

An Interlude before the Actual End

Nostalgia is one of those words that evoke the exact feeling that it is supposed to. There could never have been a different word for it. Like petrichor. It even evokes the smell. Such reminiscing is like looking at things in a rearview mirror. People, places and objects appear closer, and dearer, than what they actually are. A partial reflection of the reality sans the undesirable. Meh loved living in the past and always struggled hard to *not* keep pace with changing times. He remains that sluggish guy at the gym clutching firmly on to a treadmill handle wanting to determinedly stay where he is, as the platform of time rushes past under his feet ...

At Continental, a lot had changed. Both the other MTs had moved abroad, like their relatives. Airplanes and dhows. Sandy remained. He got a promotion too. Meh felt happy for him.

Mini *Chechi* has grown more pious; she is about to retire soon. She said she still had Meh in her prayers. Meh thanked her. The Pretty One continued to act pretty. She is Mrs Thomas now. Meh was offered the glance of a squint eye as she spoke to him for the first time, 'Did you forget us all when you have become the big-city guy?' Meh felt thankful that mannequins do not speak.

Everything else remained the same at MBL except for a new branch manager. Thomas, the bespectacled wise guy, replaced Shibu. Meh enquired about Shibu. He used to come to the branch for a few months because he had his account there. Mini *Chechi* filled Meh in. Unwilling to come to terms with his retirement, like most men in positions of power, Shibu continued to question Thomas about targets and revenues. Until one day when Thomas reminded Shibu that he was the manager and to let him handle things his way. He then showed Shibu the door ... to a trading floor where Shibu joined a thousand retired men, blended in with them and turned totally unremarkable. A mustachioed lizard on a faded yellow wall, more discreet than a fly. No one ever saw Shibu after that.

Retirement is inevitable and it is not easy for most people to come to terms with. Like death. It is always better one reconciles with it sooner and retires into a retired life, gracefully. But some still wish to remain powerful and be feared. Like a snake hoping even its shed skin evokes fear and respect. It never does. They work miserably, retire miserably, live miserably and die miserably. Hoping to be reborn; hoping to be re-employed, in a position of more power.

Meh went to the old house at Kanjikkuzhy that evening. A long desultory walk, back in time this time. A lost man searching for meanings in the dusty, mildewed memories of meaningless yesterdays. The house was locked up and looked deserted. Like it has lost its soul. Like a grandmother who has run out of stories. A banyan tree

An Interlude before the Actual End

had sprouted out of the wall cracks and grown so large, almost about to swallow the whole house. A monstrous creature willing to destroy the womb it came from. Like those feeble, innocuous thoughts that gradually grow monstrous enough to consume the very mind they came from. Meh wondered what all this meant to him. Did all these play a part in turning him into the man he is, or he is not? Does it mean anything more than being a part of a story that he may ever write? Perhaps a few pages in a book that will bring a smile as he writes, or a tear. It is all worth it. The smile, the tear, the page. Do things and people happen to us without reason or is it all scripted? Do events and people mean anything more than anecdotes and characters in a story; a story that is every man's life that may never be written about?

Finally, Meh met up with Angelo at Ambassador. The bartender smiled a familiar smile. Angelo walked in. He seemed to have aged quite a bit. He looked tired and had grown a scruffy beard—not the happy beard of a happy man, but the sad one of a sad man. Meh somehow could tell the two apart. This certainly was the sad one. Angelo had lost his wife and now lived alone. His son, like most sons in that town, was abroad. His conversations this time were mostly about loneliness and death. Again, not of a hopeful philosopher, but with a learned resignation they are all prone to at a later stage.

'I am sorry for your loss, Sir. I didn't know.'

'That is all right, Mehraz. In a way, I am kind of happy she left first. She would have never been able to live the rest of her life alone. I ... I will manage.'

'Your son?'

'Well, he has his life to live, right?'

'He sure does, but ...'

'See, when you don't have to live for anyone, you can at least die for yourself. Imagine the freedom it grants you. I am beginning to like that freedom now ... By the way, you have changed a lot; happy to see you more confident.'

Meh smiled.

'Trust me, it is always hard for human beings to change, to evolve. You know what is harder? It is harder dealing with that stubborn ape who still expects a man to behave like the ape he once was.' A stiff drink gulped down.

'Well, I don't have much of a choice now, Sir. I have loans to pay and could possibly end up getting married soon. Both not out of choice.'

'Nothing much in life is out of our choice, Mehraz. We are more the choices we do not make. Get rid of all your loans soon ... To break free of one's bondages, and mortgages, is *moksha*, you see ... so that you can be free to pursue your dreams. You had many, I remember.'

An Interlude before the Actual End

'Things change with time, don't they? I have dropped all that. But yes, I have started blogging. It gives me joy.'

'Writing! Tell me about it ... A once-aspiring writer who ended up being a pawnbroker. Those elusive dreams and inescapable realities. Life, for most people, is a fight between the two ...'

'Ah! Those two boards in your office. Always wanted to know the story behind that.'

'That is what life does to you, Mehraz. The choices that you do not make that you end up being. I am happy that you started writing. A young man, just like you, had moved from Idukki to Kottayam years ago, the hotbed of publishing those days. Hoping to be a writer, became a failed writer-publisher, eventually becoming a pawnbroker. That man might not be too happy about you wanting to write. Writing is not about writing anymore, Mehraz. Everyone talks about *best-selling*. Do you hear *good writing* being spoken of in the same way? You might as well be a salesman and sell than be a writer and be forced to sell.'

Angelo paused.

'Get a jail sentence and you will know who your true friends are, Bukowski had said; write a book, I would say. All bad men, and most good writers, have to die to be appreciated. My death will prove if I was *both*. But

I am sure you have good people around you unlike the young man from Idukki that he had to end up being a pawnbroker. Sometimes I wonder what is it that I have pawned ... My dreams, Mehraz ... My life itself.' The fourth drink downed.

'Quite encouraging, Sir.' Meh tried to laugh. He could not.

'Not that way, Mehraz. I just wanted to temper your expectations. Right now you are in that phase where you do not know what you want. No one would want you to know either, for most people do not know it *about* themselves. There are standard moulds every human will be forced to fit into. Human units on an unstoppable conveyor belt; machines with strict user manuals to adhere to. Many squeeze in and fit. They remain choked. It breaks most. Some break the mould. Then they breathe. Then they live. I wish you do, I wish everyone does. I will pray that you do. I will pray for you, Mehraz.'

'Oh, so you are also like Mini *Chechi*? Would have never guessed that. That explains the moneylender's holy faith.' Meh tried lightening the mood with a salesman's lame joke.

'Not at all; that name is only for the sake of a name, Mehraz.'

'Then? Atheist?'

'Not now, at least. I was one when I had *believed* there wasn't enough to prove the existence of anything beyond the realm of rationality. Then, I *realised* there wasn't enough to disprove such an existence, either. I am a believer today; in the good of man, in his unlimited potential for greatness, in the power of his dreams and imagination; in *everyday miracles* … And I am a firm believer in the Christianity of Christ, not of the church. Like how I can still be a communist without yielding to Red Hat Sr and his party, can't I? I pray to the same God Jesus prayed to, for we are all as much the Sons of God as he was the Son of God. Just that he had realised this truth and that made him godlike. If there is a God, I would trust Him to dwell in the deep recesses of the man he *created in his own image* and not in stone figures or buildings fashioned by a mason. The kingdom of god is within you, says the Bible. A Quranic god closer to you than your jugular. Or the Sufistic *Ana-al-Haqq* that your father can tell you about. Or the deep monistic truths contained in the *Upanishidic Mahāvākyas* that your mother may believe in. The very same truth, spoken in different languages. That truth to me is God. That realisation, my religion …'

A pause. A gulp. As if he wanted to swallow his remaining words and thoughts along with all the alcohol. As if in retaliation to how it brought it all out.

'… Tomorrow, I do not even know whether I will be interred at the church cemetery. For them, I am the heretic communist who jumped the hallowed walls of a seminary. A potential priest who became a pointless revolutionary. For the communists, I am the forsaken son of church. A failed theologian, a failed rationalist, too. I am all of these, and none of these. I am not welcomed by either groups. I don't think my body will be, too, even after I die. Death changes nothing, Mehraz …'

'A few drinks too many, Sir? I think I'll get going. I have a morning flight to catch. Maybe, we talk about all this some other day.'

'Sure, Mehraz. But remember, it is always good to have a companion in life … to share your aloneness. So that in the final stages of your life, you can at least be alone together. And if it takes a marriage for you to be with the right companion, so be it. You should get married soon, before it is too late. Why delay the good, Mehraz?'

'I'm not sure if I am ready. I'm not sure if I want to get married ever. But one thing I promise, if I do, you will be the first to be invited.'

'Stay in touch, Mehraz. You seem to be bad at it. I have lost many a good friend … to life. We all lose dear ones; sometimes to death, most of the times to life. Make sure it does not happen with you. I will wait for your wedding invitation.'

An Interlude before the Actual End

Alcohol and solitude are deadly. They can bring out the good in some, the bad in most and the truths in everyone. Together or otherwise.

It was all a bit too much for a young Mehraz to process. He realised he still missed thanking Angelo. But he did not have anymore unanswered questions. Even the unasked ones were answered. Just that they started making sense over a period of time. Like some answers that we need to grow up to. Answers that begin to make sense only when the questions die, and the questioning ceases.

A sad man with a sad beard had by then merged into the darkness of a dark town …

AND 'THE END' THAT WAS TO BE

A few more years went by. Meh changed a few jobs and cities. New places and people replaced the old ones. Some became memories. Most were forgotten. Aren't we all made of memories?—full, fragmented, forgotten.

Then, it was the season of droughts and famines, accidents and weddings. Meh was on a six-month sabbatical, his first. Sabbaticals with deadlines! He thought he would be able to figure out what was amiss. To make sense of the void that was growing within him. He could not. So he decided to get married. And to work again. So that he can take a sabbatical again.

Even god grew tired after he created man and took a day's break, says the book of Genesis: the Sabbath. Realising that this will be inadequate, then decreed for a sabbatical year once every seven years. But Meh saw that it was never easy for mortals to take a break like how god wanted; to do god things. Or perhaps it could be that we are all

And 'The End' That Was to Be

on an indefinite sabbatical. From life. A long break. A lifelong break.

The wedding invites were ready. Meh knew he had to invite Angelo. He kept delaying it. Every evening he would think of calling him, and then he would put it off for the next evening. One Monday morning Meh woke up with a strong premonition, like he had on another Monday morning—a lizard, two phone calls, swear words and an Angelo. He knew that something was to happen. Or perhaps, something has already happened. Mother reminded him it was the day to buy clothes for the wedding. Meh felt he should call Angelo. Then he thought he will do it in the evening, like the many evenings he had thought he would.

But I will have to call him today for sure. I should also thank him at the wedding in the presence of my family. Maybe that is why I could not do it any earlier. It demands a grand setting. Meh thought.

Evening. Mother was busy looking for that one outfit that would make her son the most stunning man in a crowd. She was busy rejecting cartons one after the other. Meh knew this would take an eternity. He stepped out.

Contacts: A ... An ... Ang ...

Dialling: *Angelo Sir ...*

One of the few names in Meh's contact list with any sort of honorifics attached.

An unfamiliar voice answered, 'Hello.'

'Mr Angelo?'

'*Aaraa?*' The unfamiliar voice asked Meh who he was.

That hit Meh for a brief moment. Who was he? Was he just an insurance salesman? An acquaintance? A friend? Can't be … And what was Angelo to him? Meh did not know that as well. What would he tell this man *who he was* or what Angelo was to him?

'Well, is Sir not there?'

'… Mmm … *Appa* passed away today morning. It was a cardiac arrest while he was driving to work …'

A pause.

'Hello!'

'Who's this? … Who's this? … Who's this? …'

A loud, unfamiliar voice kept repeating itself over a phone.

A louder, familiar voice kept echoing inside Meh's head.

Why delay the good, Mehraz …

(Inspired by real life. Inspired by real humans.)

A THANK-YOU NOTE (CONTINUED)

We all have Angelos in our lives. Ones who come from nowhere, do their angelic bit, before vanishing to nowhere. Not waiting for a word of gratitude, or even a goodbye. Sometimes forcing us to write a whole book instead of that one 'thank you' we missed to say in time. Without further ado …

… dedicating this one to my Angelo here before it gets any later. Thank you, dear Sir.

To all my readers who trusted an unknown author and his first book—that first cheque to a rookie salesman. Now his second, too. Thank you, before it is too late again.

Thanking Balambika, Reji and Prachi for prodding me to attempt humour and a lighter read. My attempted poetry and writing about life was not funny enough for some.

It would have taken a long time if not for a confused stray that bit me on my birthday, for no reason. I never saw her appear or disappear. Only saw her look at me apologetically after biting. *Damn! The wrong guy, again.* She then let go, of the bite. And dissolved into fairy dust. Poof! Only a wound remains.

Thanks to an equally apologetic doctor who was as confused as the dog and I. Any doctor doing math, or asking you to trust in God for things to work, can be scary. 'There is no way for you to know if the vaccines have worked or if you've got the virus. In case if you get it, there is no use knowing and then, you have had it.'

Foreboding words. It made me act. It made me write. A will. A manuscript. All in ten days. What would have taken at least ten years in my regular lazy course.

Thank you, everyone. Everyone, who is an Angelo to someone.

Rasal
15 December, 2022

POSTSCRIPT

- Angelo's family took out the claim after about a month, Sandy confirmed. The noblest part of any insurer's job, the most painful too. That one product a seller wishes the buyer never has a need to use.
- Sandy still works with Continental. The only MT who remains, he is now the territory manager. Not the CEO, just yet.
- The then territory manager is now one of the closest people in Meh's life. Close enough to share a beer and return the *theris*.
- Continental stopped offering MT program in India from the following year.
- There were more Angelos who helped Mehraz build his career. Bigger cheques, celebratory cake cuttings continued.
- All of them brought back memories of a Rs 29,279 cheque. None appeared as big or evoked the same joy. No *bigger* deal!
- Mehraz remained Meh for a long time trying to figure out what was amiss.

Postscript

- He took that second sabbatical and went on to write a book, making sense of all the void finally. (https://www.amazon.in/Killed-Golden-Goose-COLLECTION-THOUGHTLESSNESS/dp/163940483X)
- He dropped the *Meh* totally, becoming more of Rasal: his 'demi-writer' father.
- He then wrote a book titled *No Bigg Deal!* An incidental prequel to an unintended sequel.
- He believes he now has the answer to what Angelo was to him and hopes to hand over a copy of the book to Angelo's family.

A phonebook entry with an honorific remains undeleted.

End of story.

For reviews/refunds (guaranteed this time): theunreadone@gmail.com

Or,

Until the next book we meet ...

Cheers!

ABOUT THE AUTHOR

Rasal is a writer when he is absolutely sure there is a story worth sharing. Otherwise, he spends his time idling, dreaming, reading and travelling. In his former avatar, he was a Vice President at Goldman Sachs before he published his first book, *I Killed the Golden Goose*. A book for those at life's crossroads torn between passions and professions, hearts and heads; between undreamt dreams and unpaid mortgages.

The reassuring responses from his readers helped him be less confused about the path ahead. He made 'life's first unforced choice' as he entered the world of books and literature following his father, the *demi-writer*, and his grandfather, the unschooled village bard.

Rasal is happy sharing his stories with anyone who is happy to be shared with. He then goes back to being that obscure man of few words as the idling resumes.

And, the dreaming begins …

Made in the USA
Monee, IL
03 May 2026

49438949R00090